How to Design
Your Own Sigils for
Everyday Magic:
A Practical Workbook

Selvaggio, Ana Maria

How to Design Your Own Sigils for Everyday Magic
by Ana Maria Selvaggio

ISBN-13: 978-1-7345104-9-2
ISBN-10: 1-7345104-9-8

1.   BODY, MIND & SPIRIT / Numerology
2.   SELF-HELP / Self-Management / General
3.   SELF-HELP / Personal Growth / Self-Esteem

For inquiries about volume orders, please contact:
dflypress@gmail.com

Ana Maria Selvaggio
Renmeleon
www.renmeleon.com

Published in the United States by Dragonfly Press Publishing
Distributed by Renmeleon
Cover & Interior by Ana Maria Selvaggio | Renmeleon.com

10 9 8 7 6 5 4 3 2 1
Printed in the United States of America

Introduction

As a creative, I know that many of us will get hyperfocused on birthing new projects or investing in our everyday work to the point of forgetting to eat and take breaks. As a creative who deals with ADD on a daily basis, everything needs to be in my line of sight for it to be functional. I started using visual cues as a way to remind myself to work my own wellness into my everyday life.

Sigils, for the purpose of this method, are personal symbols designed to give you pause and refocus your day-to-day on the areas you need to work on most - personal wellness, goals, and the things that are important to you.

It is my hope that using sigils in your everyday life will remind you that magic is everywhere and that you have the power to shape both your internal and external environments.

Brightest blessings,

How to Use This Workbook

The first section of this workbook will walk you through creating a personal sigil step-by-step.

The remaining pages consist of two-page spreads for each sigil where you can design and record the sigils you make. Designing a sigil is as simple as following the prompts on each page.

Sigils can be drawn on paper, on sticky notes, on sticker paper, or even painted on surfaces. Utilize your own sigil wherever you need a reminder or prompt for thought. There are enough spreads included for 100 sigils and an index in the very back to record what page number each is on.

Enjoy!

Disclaimer: I am a firm believer that what you put out comes back to you, tenfold. Sigils should never be used with the intent to harm or wish ill will on others or yourself. The intent of this book is to instruct you on how to create and use your own sigils for positive affirmation and action.

Sigils have been used for centuries. Originating in ritual magic, they also have a more straight-forward, modern, practical application.

For modern use, sigils are a consolidation of intentions formed into one single symbol. We have taken to creating them for a variety of uses around our home as reminders or triggers for things we need to make important or for use on gifts. This way of making sigils utilizes Numerology as a translation tool.

There are two ways to make sigils that I will show examples of. The process is the same, but one is keyword based, while the other is a sentence. Keep the steps the same, but make this your process.

Numerology

Numerology is heavily used in Astrology, for birth charts, and in other forms of divination. My father, however, used it in more practical ways.

In Numerology, the letters of the alphabet are given numerical associations from 1 to 9. From there, words are then converted to create meaning in a different way. For making sigils, it is a way to help narrow down and distill your intentions.

Write your intention

On a piece of paper, make a list of words that form your intention. For example, to make a sigil for my houseplants...yes, I'm that person...I thought about what I wanted the sigil for: I wanted my plants to grow, be healthy and, in the case of my herbs and food-bearing plants, yield nutrition. Since making sigils works better with fewer words, I came up with this list, then narrowed it down a bit...

Growth
~~Nourishment~~
Strength
Longevity
Abundance
Fruitfulness
~~Blessed~~
Good health

Distillation

Fruitful became *fruitfulness* and I double-checked the definition: "Extremely productive and prolific." according to Merriam-Webster. It is very important to have clear intentions and use the right words. In the end I had six words; technically seven since one is two words. A little long but it felt right, it felt *whole*.

Growth
Strength
Longevity
Abundance
Fruitfulness
Good health

The next steps should be done with thought and accuracy. Take it slow. Start thinking of how each word will manifest itself as you follow these next steps. This is action with *intention*.

1. Cross out all of the vowels. Using my word list above...

grwth
strngth
lngvt
bndnc
frtflnss
gd hlth

2. Cross out all repeated letters keeping the first of each letter...

grwth
sn
lv
bdc
f

3. Convert the letters to numbers then cross out repeats. Once you assigned a number to each letter, keep the first presentation of the number and remove the duplicates. It is very important to do this in order.

1	2	3	4	5	6	7	8	9
A	B	C	D	E	F	G	H	I
J	K	L	M	N	O	P	Q	R
S	T	U	V	W	X	Y	Z	

grwth sn lv bdc
becomes 7952834243
then 952834

These next steps can be done by hand on paper. Hand drawing and hand painting your sigils are a way to connect with them further. I take mine digital to make them into rubber stamps, wax seals for letters, stickers, and for other uses like in my signature.

As an example of use, the sigil on the cover and at the beginning of the book means:

"Bless this space (yours) with wellness, abundance, and protection so kindness, love, and patience prevail."

Going Digital

If you do decide to create a digital file that you can export, there are several places online where you can create products for yourself. Maybe make a mug with a productive day + protection sigil? A blanket with a repeat pattern of restful sleep sigils? Look for POD or "print on demand" sites that offer product customization like Zazzle or, for fabric, like Spoonflower.

Simplifying the Process

Setting up a simple chart will streamline things for you, especially if you plan to make sigils on a regular basis. Word of warning: Making sigils is like getting a new label maker, you're going to want to put them *everywhere*.

Make a 3 x 3 grid of squares that looks like a tic-tac-toe board but with a dot in the center of each square and numbers out of the way in the top left corner of each square. You will use this in the next steps.

Mapping it

Draw your sigil using the numbers in step 3, making sure to go in order. Draw a small round dot in the middle of the first number's square. From that first number, draw a straight line to the next number then to the next and so on till you have connected the points like a dot-to-dot to all of the numbers. From there, you have your sigil and you can stylize it however you like.

The one I created for my plants can be written on the inside bottom of a new flower pot before I plant something in it. For the ones already in pots, I can draw it on the bottom of the pot or get decorative and paint it on the outside of the pot. Whatever feels right. *Make your sigil your own.*

Here is the sigil for my plants again with the words so you can see the correlations...

Journaling your intentions

One of the things that I have enjoyed doing as part of the process, the same as I do when I do tarot or oracle readings, is journaling my intentions. To this purpose I have included two pages after each sigil section to be used for journaling if you wish. If not, it can be used as scratch paper to hone your intention phrasing. I find it useful to look back on why I created a sigil, what its story is and, if done in pencil, modify it later. I create my sigils and journal about them so I remember the purpose they were created for. As a bookbinder, I love making my own tea or coffee-stained pages to bind them. It adds to the intention and just makes it feel more sacred to me.

One last note: I am not a fan of "resolutions". I set goals and break them down into baby steps. I set reminders with sigils to keep things in my line of sight, I do not use sigils for specific tasks. They are intentions already in progress that I renew daily every time I see them.

Forms and Function

Use your imagination and look around you. What is the routine path around your home, we all have one. Where could you put sigils that would be in your line of sight? What would work best for you - sticky notes, actual stickers, your new favorite coffee mug? Placement will affect form so take a moment and think about your environment each time you create one and make each sigil personal.

Now Get Going, You Got This

Drop me a note @Renmeleon on any social medium if you share your sigils. I would love to see them. Be brightly blessed!

MY PERSONAL
SIGILS

Write your intention
Make a list of words that form your intention.

Love

Abundance

HEALTH

Distillation (optional)
Rewrite your words with clear intentions into a short, concise sentence.

I AM LOVED

I AM ABUNDENT

I AM HEALTHY

*With thought and accuracy, think of how each word
will manifest itself as you follow these next steps.
This is action with intention. Take it slow.*

1. Cross out all of the vowels in your words/sentence. Write what is left
here, making sure to keep them in their order.

M LVD

MBNDNT

M HLTH

2. Cross out any repeated letters; keep the first of each letter but remove
any duplicates.

M LVD

BNT

H

3. Convert the letters to numbers then cross out any repeated numbers.
Once you assign a number to each letter, keep the first presentation of
the number and remove the duplicates. It is very important to do this
in order.

1	2	3	4	5	6	7	8	9
A	B	C	D	E	F	G	H	I
J	K	L	M	N	O	P	Q	R
S	T	U	V	W	X	Y	Z	

4 3 4 4 2 5 2 8

4 3 2 5 8

14

Map It
Draw a large dot in the center of the first number to mark the beginning of your intent, then draw a line through every number's center point in the chart below in the order they appear in your number.

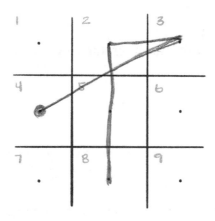

Done! Now Practice
Hone the shape into what suits you best, just make sure to do the points in order and speak your manifestation as you draw it.

volwels –

a, e, i, o, u, y

Write your intention
Make a list of words that form your intention.

_____

_____

_____

Distillation (optional)
Rewrite your words with clear intentions into a short, concise sentence.

_____

_____

_____

With thought and accuracy, think of how each word
will manifest itself as you follow these next steps.
This is action with intention. Take it slow.

1. Cross out all of the vowels in your words/sentence. Write what is left here, making sure to keep them in their order.

_____   _____

_____   _____

_____   _____

2. Cross out any repeated letters; keep the first of each letter but remove any duplicates.

_____   _____

_____   _____

_____   _____

3. Convert the letters to numbers then cross out any repeated numbers. Once you assign a number to each letter, keep the first presentation of the number and remove the duplicates. It is very important to do this in order.

1	2	3	4	5	6	7	8	9
A	B	C	D	E	F	G	H	I
J	K	L	M	N	O	P	Q	R
S	T	U	V	W	X	Y	Z	

_____

Map It

Draw a large dot in the center of the first number to mark the beginning of your intent, then draw a line through every number's center point in the chart below in the order they appear in your number.

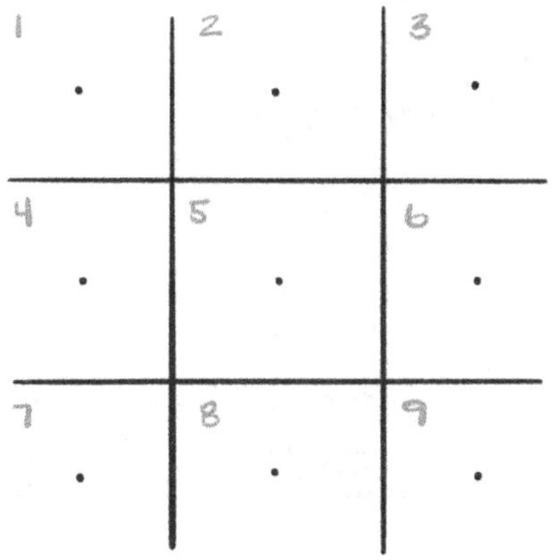

Done! Now Practice

Hone the shape into what suits you best, just make sure to do the points in order and speak your manifestation as you draw it.

Write your intention
Make a list of words that form your intention.

_____

_____

_____

Distillation (optional)
Rewrite your words with clear intentions into a short, concise sentence.

_____

_____

_____

With thought and accuracy, think of how each word
will manifest itself as you follow these next steps.
This is action with intention. Take it slow.

1. Cross out all of the vowels in your words/sentence. Write what is left here, making sure to keep them in their order.

_____   _____

_____   _____

_____   _____

2. Cross out any repeated letters; keep the first of each letter but remove any duplicates.

_____   _____

_____   _____

_____   _____

3. Convert the letters to numbers then cross out any repeated numbers. Once you assign a number to each letter, keep the first presentation of the number and remove the duplicates. It is very important to do this in order.

1	2	3	4	5	6	7	8	9
A	B	C	D	E	F	G	H	I
J	K	L	M	N	O	P	Q	R
S	T	U	V	W	X	Y	Z	

_____

Map It

Draw a large dot in the center of the first number to mark the beginning of your intent, then draw a line through every number's center point in the chart below in the order they appear in your number.

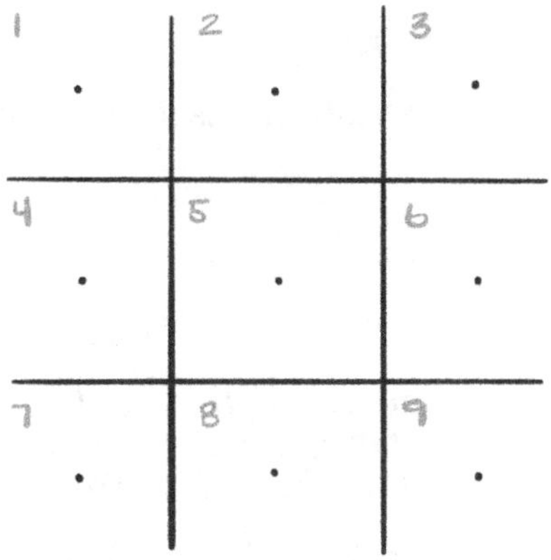

Done! Now Practice

Hone the shape into what suits you best, just make sure to do the points in order and speak your manifestation as you draw it.

Write your intention
Make a list of words that form your intention.

_____

_____

_____

Distillation (optional)
Rewrite your words with clear intentions into a short, concise sentence.

_____

_____

_____

With thought and accuracy, think of how each word
will manifest itself as you follow these next steps.
This is action with intention. Take it slow.

1. Cross out all of the vowels in your words/sentence. Write what is left here, making sure to keep them in their order.

_____   _____

_____   _____

_____   _____

2. Cross out any repeated letters; keep the first of each letter but remove any duplicates.

_____   _____

_____   _____

_____   _____

3. Convert the letters to numbers then cross out any repeated numbers. Once you assign a number to each letter, keep the first presentation of the number and remove the duplicates. It is very important to do this in order.

1	2	3	4	5	6	7	8	9
A	B	C	D	E	F	G	H	I
J	K	L	M	N	O	P	Q	R
S	T	U	V	W	X	Y	Z	

_____

Map It
Draw a large dot in the center of the first number to mark the beginning
of your intent, then draw a line through every number's center point in
the chart below in the order they appear in your number.

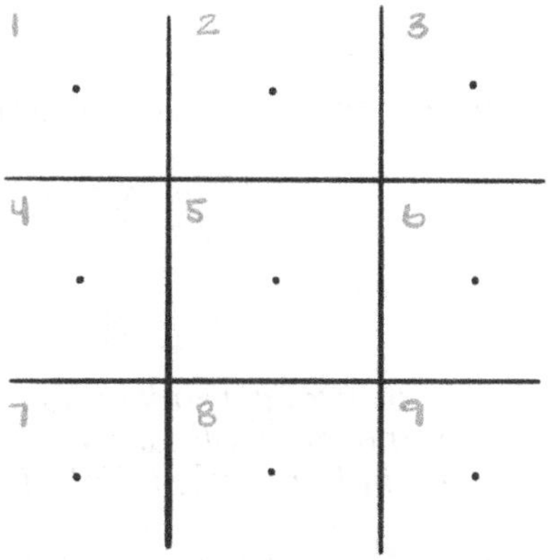

Done! Now Practice
Hone the shape into what suits you best, just make sure to do the points
in order and speak your manifestation as you draw it.

Write your intention
Make a list of words that form your intention.

_____

_____

_____

Distillation (optional)
Rewrite your words with clear intentions into a short, concise sentence.

_____

_____

_____

*With thought and accuracy, think of how each word
will manifest itself as you follow these next steps.
This is action with intention. Take it slow.*

1. Cross out all of the vowels in your words/sentence. Write what is left here, making sure to keep them in their order.

_____   _____

_____   _____

_____   _____

2. Cross out any repeated letters; keep the first of each letter but remove any duplicates.

_____   _____

_____   _____

_____   _____

3. Convert the letters to numbers then cross out any repeated numbers. Once you assign a number to each letter, keep the first presentation of the number and remove the duplicates. It is very important to do this in order.

1	2	3	4	5	6	7	8	9
A	B	C	D	E	F	G	H	I
J	K	L	M	N	O	P	Q	R
S	T	U	V	W	X	Y	Z	

_____

22

Map It
Draw a large dot in the center of the first number to mark the beginning of your intent, then draw a line through every number's center point in the chart below in the order they appear in your number.

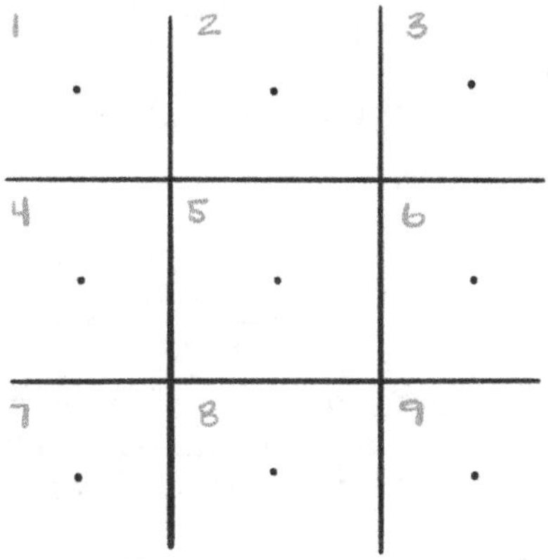

```
  1  │   2   │  3
   •  │    •  │    •
─────┼───────┼─────
  4  │   5   │  6
   •  │    •  │    •
─────┼───────┼─────
  7  │   8   │  9
   •  │    •  │    •
```

Done! Now Practice
Hone the shape into what suits you best, just make sure to do the points in order and speak your manifestation as you draw it.

Write your intention
Make a list of words that form your intention.

_____

_____

_____

Distillation (optional)
Rewrite your words with clear intentions into a short, concise sentence.

_____

_____

_____

With thought and accuracy, think of how each word
will manifest itself as you follow these next steps.
This is action with intention. Take it slow.

1. Cross out all of the vowels in your words/sentence. Write what is left here, making sure to keep them in their order.

_____   _____

_____   _____

_____   _____

2. Cross out any repeated letters; keep the first of each letter but remove any duplicates.

_____   _____

_____   _____

_____   _____

3. Convert the letters to numbers then cross out any repeated numbers. Once you assign a number to each letter, keep the first presentation of the number and remove the duplicates. It is very important to do this in order.

1	2	3	4	5	6	7	8	9
A	B	C	D	E	F	G	H	I
J	K	L	M	N	O	P	Q	R
S	T	U	V	W	X	Y	Z	

_____

Map It

Draw a large dot in the center of the first number to mark the beginning of your intent, then draw a line through every number's center point in the chart below in the order they appear in your number.

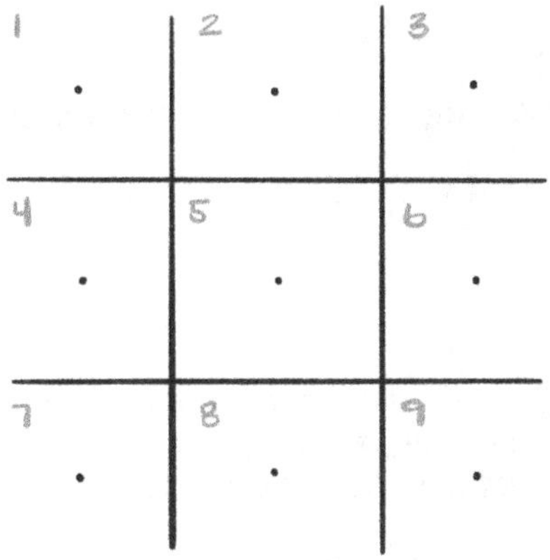

Done! Now Practice

Hone the shape into what suits you best, just make sure to do the points in order and speak your manifestation as you draw it.

Write your intention
Make a list of words that form your intention.

_____

_____

_____

Distillation (optional)
Rewrite your words with clear intentions into a short, concise sentence.

_____

_____

_____

With thought and accuracy, think of how each word
will manifest itself as you follow these next steps.
This is action with intention. Take it slow.

1. Cross out all of the vowels in your words/sentence. Write what is left here, making sure to keep them in their order.

_____   _____

_____   _____

_____   _____

2. Cross out any repeated letters; keep the first of each letter but remove any duplicates.

_____   _____

_____   _____

_____   _____

3. Convert the letters to numbers then cross out any repeated numbers. Once you assign a number to each letter, keep the first presentation of the number and remove the duplicates. It is very important to do this in order.

1	2	3	4	5	6	7	8	9
A	B	C	D	E	F	G	H	I
J	K	L	M	N	O	P	Q	R
S	T	U	V	W	X	Y	Z	

_____

Map It
Draw a large dot in the center of the first number to mark the beginning
of your intent, then draw a line through every number's center point in
the chart below in the order they appear in your number.

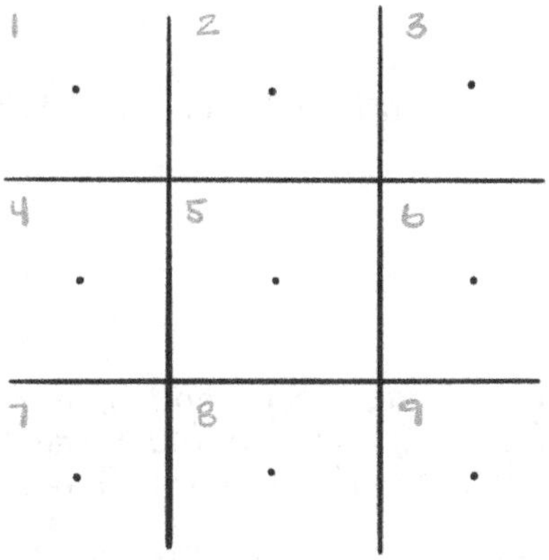

Done! Now Practice
Hone the shape into what suits you best, just make sure to do the points
in order and speak your manifestation as you draw it.

Write your intention
Make a list of words that form your intention.

_____

_____

_____

Distillation (optional)
Rewrite your words with clear intentions into a short, concise sentence.

_____

_____

_____

*With thought and accuracy, think of how each word
will manifest itself as you follow these next steps.
This is action with intention. Take it slow.*

1. Cross out all of the vowels in your words/sentence. Write what is left
here, making sure to keep them in their order.

_____   _____

_____   _____

_____   _____

2. Cross out any repeated letters; keep the first of each letter but remove
any duplicates.

_____   _____

_____   _____

_____   _____

3. Convert the letters to numbers then cross out any repeated numbers.
Once you assign a number to each letter, keep the first presentation of
the number and remove the duplicates. It is very important to do this
in order.

1	2	3	4	5	6	7	8	9
A	B	C	D	E	F	G	H	I
J	K	L	M	N	O	P	Q	R
S	T	U	V	W	X	Y	Z	

_____

Map It
Draw a large dot in the center of the first number to mark the beginning of your intent, then draw a line through every number's center point in the chart below in the order they appear in your number.

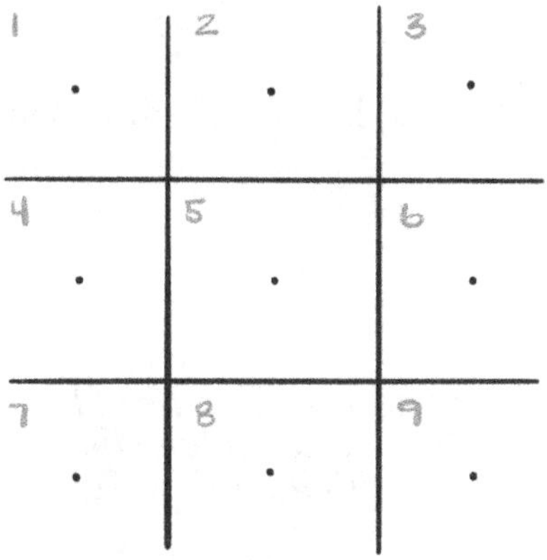

Done! Now Practice
Hone the shape into what suits you best, just make sure to do the points in order and speak your manifestation as you draw it.

Write your intention
Make a list of words that form your intention.

_____

_____

_____

Distillation (optional)
Rewrite your words with clear intentions into a short, concise sentence.

_____

_____

_____

With thought and accuracy, think of how each word
will manifest itself as you follow these next steps.
This is action with intention. Take it slow.

1. Cross out all of the vowels in your words/sentence. Write what is left here, making sure to keep them in their order.

_____   _____

_____   _____

_____   _____

2. Cross out any repeated letters; keep the first of each letter but remove any duplicates.

_____   _____

_____   _____

_____   _____

3. Convert the letters to numbers then cross out any repeated numbers. Once you assign a number to each letter, keep the first presentation of the number and remove the duplicates. It is very important to do this in order.

1	2	3	4	5	6	7	8	9
A	B	C	D	E	F	G	H	I
J	K	L	M	N	O	P	Q	R
S	T	U	V	W	X	Y	Z	

_____

Map It
Draw a large dot in the center of the first number to mark the beginning of your intent, then draw a line through every number's center point in the chart below in the order they appear in your number.

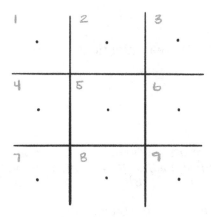

Done! Now Practice
Hone the shape into what suits you best, just make sure to do the points in order and speak your manifestation as you draw it.

Write your intention
Make a list of words that form your intention.

_____

_____

_____

Distillation (optional)
Rewrite your words with clear intentions into a short, concise sentence.

_____

_____

_____

With thought and accuracy, think of how each word
will manifest itself as you follow these next steps.
This is action with intention. Take it slow.

1. Cross out all of the vowels in your words/sentence. Write what is left here, making sure to keep them in their order.

_____   _____

_____   _____

_____   _____

2. Cross out any repeated letters; keep the first of each letter but remove any duplicates.

_____   _____

_____   _____

_____   _____

3. Convert the letters to numbers then cross out any repeated numbers. Once you assign a number to each letter, keep the first presentation of the number and remove the duplicates. It is very important to do this in order.

1	2	3	4	5	6	7	8	9
A	B	C	D	E	F	G	H	I
J	K	L	M	N	O	P	Q	R
S	T	U	V	W	X	Y	Z	

_____

Map It
Draw a large dot in the center of the first number to mark the beginning
of your intent, then draw a line through every number's center point in
the chart below in the order they appear in your number.

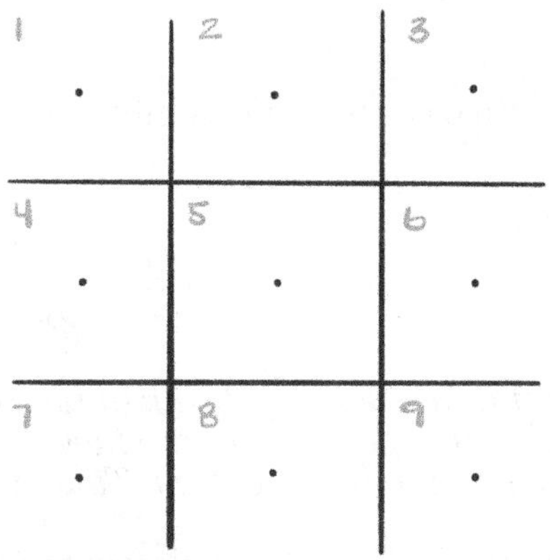

1	2	3
•	•	•
4	5	6
•	•	•
7	8	9
•	•	•

Done! Now Practice
Hone the shape into what suits you best, just make sure to do the points
in order and speak your manifestation as you draw it.

Write your intention
Make a list of words that form your intention.

_____

_____

_____

Distillation (optional)
Rewrite your words with clear intentions into a short, concise sentence.

_____

_____

_____

With thought and accuracy, think of how each word
will manifest itself as you follow these next steps.
This is action with intention. Take it slow.

1. Cross out all of the vowels in your words/sentence. Write what is left here, making sure to keep them in their order.

_____   _____

_____   _____

_____   _____

2. Cross out any repeated letters; keep the first of each letter but remove any duplicates.

_____   _____

_____   _____

_____   _____

3. Convert the letters to numbers then cross out any repeated numbers. Once you assign a number to each letter, keep the first presentation of the number and remove the duplicates. It is very important to do this in order.

1	2	3	4	5	6	7	8	9
A	B	C	D	E	F	G	H	I
J	K	L	M	N	O	P	Q	R
S	T	U	V	W	X	Y	Z	

_____

Map It
Draw a large dot in the center of the first number to mark the beginning of your intent, then draw a line through every number's center point in the chart below in the order they appear in your number.

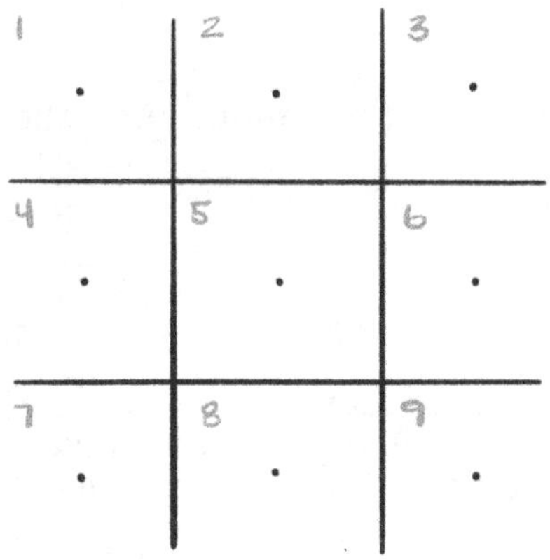

Done! Now Practice
Hone the shape into what suits you best, just make sure to do the points in order and speak your manifestation as you draw it.

Write your intention
Make a list of words that form your intention.

_____

_____

_____

Distillation (optional)
Rewrite your words with clear intentions into a short, concise sentence.

_____

_____

_____

With thought and accuracy, think of how each word
will manifest itself as you follow these next steps.
This is action with intention. Take it slow.

1. Cross out all of the vowels in your words/sentence. Write what is left here, making sure to keep them in their order.

_____   _____

_____   _____

_____   _____

2. Cross out any repeated letters; keep the first of each letter but remove any duplicates.

_____   _____

_____   _____

_____   _____

3. Convert the letters to numbers then cross out any repeated numbers. Once you assign a number to each letter, keep the first presentation of the number and remove the duplicates. It is very important to do this in order.

1	2	3	4	5	6	7	8	9
A	B	C	D	E	F	G	H	I
J	K	L	M	N	O	P	Q	R
S	T	U	V	W	X	Y	Z	

_____

Map It
Draw a large dot in the center of the first number to mark the beginning of your intent, then draw a line through every number's center point in the chart below in the order they appear in your number.

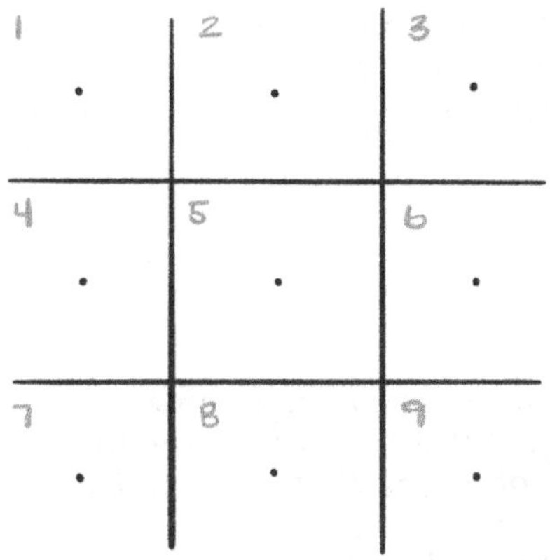

Done! Now Practice
Hone the shape into what suits you best, just make sure to do the points in order and speak your manifestation as you draw it.

Write your intention
Make a list of words that form your intention.

_____

_____

_____

Distillation (optional)
Rewrite your words with clear intentions into a short, concise sentence.

_____

_____

_____

With thought and accuracy, think of how each word
will manifest itself as you follow these next steps.
This is action with intention. Take it slow.

1. Cross out all of the vowels in your words/sentence. Write what is left
here, making sure to keep them in their order.

_____   _____

_____   _____

_____   _____

2. Cross out any repeated letters; keep the first of each letter but remove
any duplicates.

_____   _____

_____   _____

_____   _____

3. Convert the letters to numbers then cross out any repeated numbers.
Once you assign a number to each letter, keep the first presentation of
the number and remove the duplicates. It is very important to do this
in order.

1	2	3	4	5	6	7	8	9
A	B	C	D	E	F	G	H	I
J	K	L	M	N	O	P	Q	R
S	T	U	V	W	X	Y	Z	

_____

Map It

Draw a large dot in the center of the first number to mark the beginning of your intent, then draw a line through every number's center point in the chart below in the order they appear in your number.

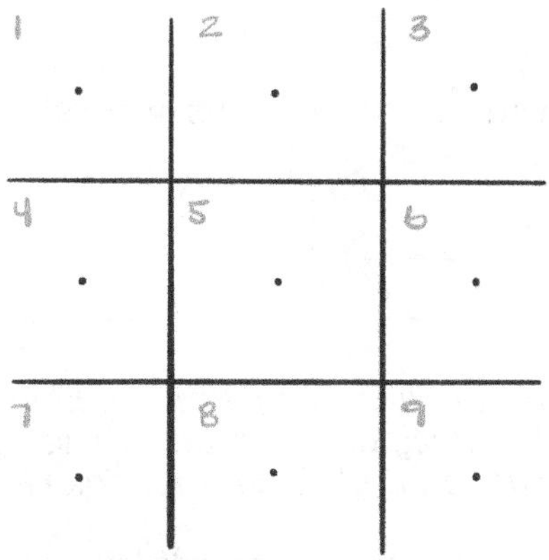

Done! Now Practice

Hone the shape into what suits you best, just make sure to do the points in order and speak your manifestation as you draw it.

Write your intention
Make a list of words that form your intention.

_____

_____

_____

Distillation (optional)
Rewrite your words with clear intentions into a short, concise sentence.

_____

_____

_____

*With thought and accuracy, think of how each word
will manifest itself as you follow these next steps.
This is action with intention. Take it slow.*

1. Cross out all of the vowels in your words/sentence. Write what is left here, making sure to keep them in their order.

_____   _____

_____   _____

_____   _____

2. Cross out any repeated letters; keep the first of each letter but remove any duplicates.

_____   _____

_____   _____

_____   _____

3. Convert the letters to numbers then cross out any repeated numbers. Once you assign a number to each letter, keep the first presentation of the number and remove the duplicates. It is very important to do this in order.

1	2	3	4	5	6	7	8	9
A	B	C	D	E	F	G	H	I
J	K	L	M	N	O	P	Q	R
S	T	U	V	W	X	Y	Z	

_____

Map It
Draw a large dot in the center of the first number to mark the beginning of your intent, then draw a line through every number's center point in the chart below in the order they appear in your number.

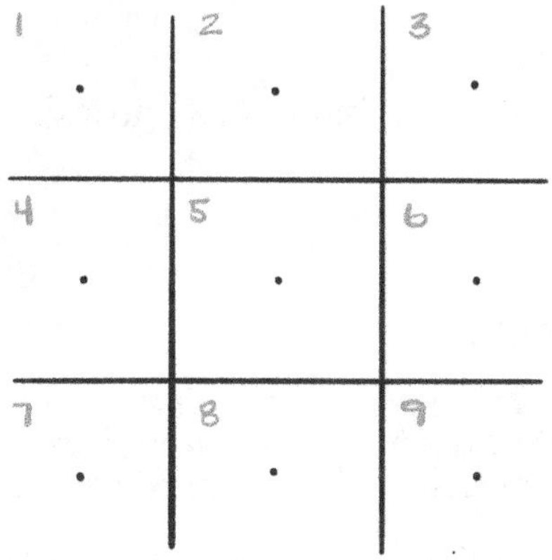

1	2	3
4	5	6
7	8	9

Done! Now Practice
Hone the shape into what suits you best, just make sure to do the points in order and speak your manifestation as you draw it.

Write your intention
Make a list of words that form your intention.

_____

_____

_____

Distillation (optional)
Rewrite your words with clear intentions into a short, concise sentence.

_____

_____

_____

With thought and accuracy, think of how each word
will manifest itself as you follow these next steps.
This is action with intention. Take it slow.

1. Cross out all of the vowels in your words/sentence. Write what is left here, making sure to keep them in their order.

_____   _____

_____   _____

_____   _____

2. Cross out any repeated letters; keep the first of each letter but remove any duplicates.

_____   _____

_____   _____

_____   _____

3. Convert the letters to numbers then cross out any repeated numbers. Once you assign a number to each letter, keep the first presentation of the number and remove the duplicates. It is very important to do this in order.

1	2	3	4	5	6	7	8	9
A	B	C	D	E	F	G	H	I
J	K	L	M	N	O	P	Q	R
S	T	U	V	W	X	Y	Z	

_____

Map It

Draw a large dot in the center of the first number to mark the beginning of your intent, then draw a line through every number's center point in the chart below in the order they appear in your number.

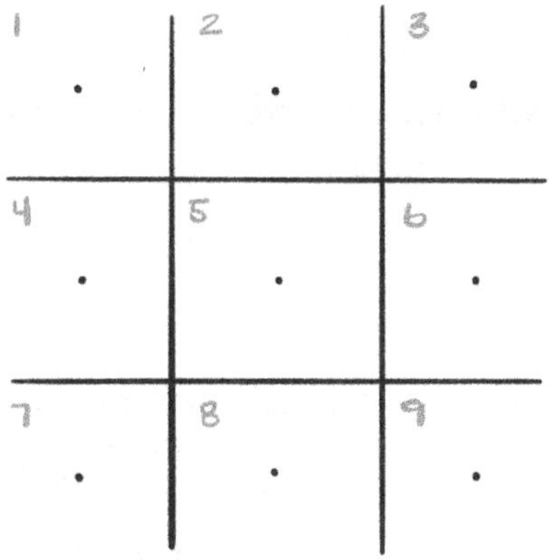

Done! Now Practice

Hone the shape into what suits you best, just make sure to do the points in order and speak your manifestation as you draw it.

Write your intention
Make a list of words that form your intention.

_____

_____

_____

Distillation (optional)
Rewrite your words with clear intentions into a short, concise sentence.

_____

_____

_____

*With thought and accuracy, think of how each word
will manifest itself as you follow these next steps.
This is action with intention. Take it slow.*

1. Cross out all of the vowels in your words/sentence. Write what is left
here, making sure to keep them in their order.

_____   _____

_____   _____

_____   _____

2. Cross out any repeated letters; keep the first of each letter but remove
any duplicates.

_____   _____

_____   _____

_____   _____

3. Convert the letters to numbers then cross out any repeated numbers.
Once you assign a number to each letter, keep the first presentation of
the number and remove the duplicates. It is very important to do this
in order.

1	2	3	4	5	6	7	8	9
A	B	C	D	E	F	G	H	I
J	K	L	M	N	O	P	Q	R
S	T	U	V	W	X	Y	Z	

_____

Map It

Draw a large dot in the center of the first number to mark the beginning of your intent, then draw a line through every number's center point in the chart below in the order they appear in your number.

1	2	3
.	.	.
4	5	6
.	.	.
7	8	9
.	.	.

Done! Now Practice

Hone the shape into what suits you best, just make sure to do the points in order and speak your manifestation as you draw it.

Write your intention
Make a list of words that form your intention.

Distillation (optional)
Rewrite your words with clear intentions into a short, concise sentence.

With thought and accuracy, think of how each word
will manifest itself as you follow these next steps.
This is action with intention. Take it slow.

1. Cross out all of the vowels in your words/sentence. Write what is left here, making sure to keep them in their order.

---

2. Cross out any repeated letters; keep the first of each letter but remove any duplicates.

---

3. Convert the letters to numbers then cross out any repeated numbers. Once you assign a number to each letter, keep the first presentation of the number and remove the duplicates. It is very important to do this in order.

1	2	3	4	5	6	7	8	9
A	B	C	D	E	F	G	H	I
J	K	L	M	N	O	P	Q	R
S	T	U	V	W	X	Y	Z	

Map It

Draw a large dot in the center of the first number to mark the beginning of your intent, then draw a line through every number's center point in the chart below in the order they appear in your number.

1 ·	2 ·	3 ·
4 ·	5 ·	6 ·
7 ·	8 ·	9 ·

Done! Now Practice

Hone the shape into what suits you best, just make sure to do the points in order and speak your manifestation as you draw it.

Write your intention
Make a list of words that form your intention.

_____

_____

_____

Distillation (optional)
Rewrite your words with clear intentions into a short, concise sentence.

_____

_____

_____

*With thought and accuracy, think of how each word
will manifest itself as you follow these next steps.
This is action with intention. Take it slow.*

1. Cross out all of the vowels in your words/sentence. Write what is left
here, making sure to keep them in their order.

_____   _____

_____   _____

_____   _____

2. Cross out any repeated letters; keep the first of each letter but remove
any duplicates.

_____   _____

_____   _____

_____   _____

3. Convert the letters to numbers then cross out any repeated numbers.
Once you assign a number to each letter, keep the first presentation of
the number and remove the duplicates. It is very important to do this
in order.

1	2	3	4	5	6	7	8	9
A	B	C	D	E	F	G	H	I
J	K	L	M	N	O	P	Q	R
S	T	U	V	W	X	Y	Z	

_____

48

Map It

Draw a large dot in the center of the first number to mark the beginning of your intent, then draw a line through every number's center point in the chart below in the order they appear in your number.

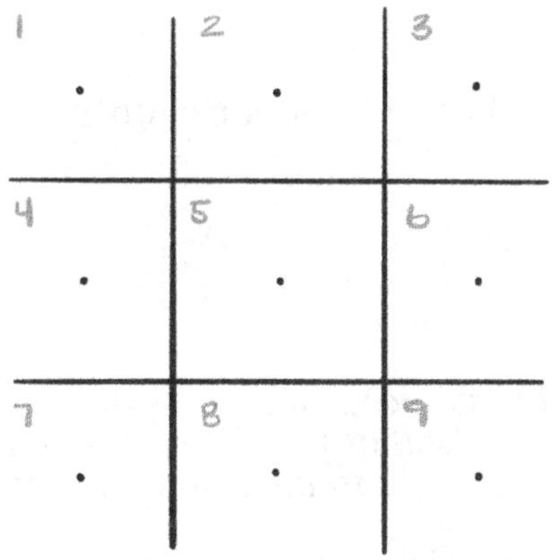

Done! Now Practice

Hone the shape into what suits you best, just make sure to do the points in order and speak your manifestation as you draw it.

Write your intention
Make a list of words that form your intention.

_____

_____

_____

Distillation (optional)
Rewrite your words with clear intentions into a short, concise sentence.

_____

_____

_____

With thought and accuracy, think of how each word
will manifest itself as you follow these next steps.
This is action with intention. Take it slow.

1. Cross out all of the vowels in your words/sentence. Write what is left here, making sure to keep them in their order.

_____   _____

_____   _____

_____   _____

2. Cross out any repeated letters; keep the first of each letter but remove any duplicates.

_____   _____

_____   _____

_____   _____

3. Convert the letters to numbers then cross out any repeated numbers. Once you assign a number to each letter, keep the first presentation of the number and remove the duplicates. It is very important to do this in order.

1	2	3	4	5	6	7	8	9
A	B	C	D	E	F	G	H	I
J	K	L	M	N	O	P	Q	R
S	T	U	V	W	X	Y	Z	

_____

Map It

Draw a large dot in the center of the first number to mark the beginning of your intent, then draw a line through every number's center point in the chart below in the order they appear in your number.

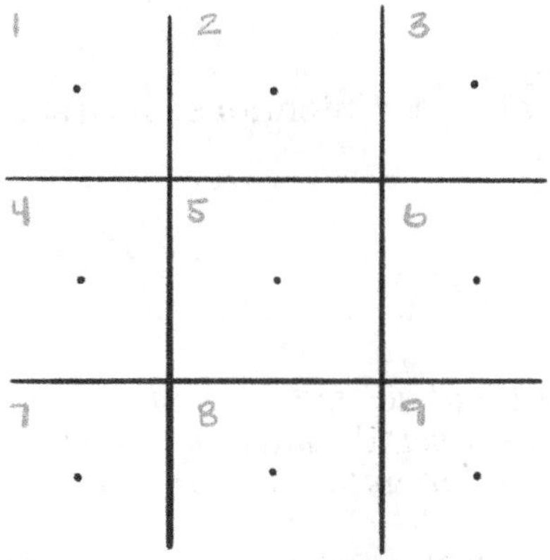

Done! Now Practice

Hone the shape into what suits you best, just make sure to do the points in order and speak your manifestation as you draw it.

Write your intention
Make a list of words that form your intention.

_____

_____

_____

Distillation (optional)
Rewrite your words with clear intentions into a short, concise sentence.

_____

_____

_____

*With thought and accuracy, think of how each word
will manifest itself as you follow these next steps.
This is action with intention. Take it slow.*

1. Cross out all of the vowels in your words/sentence. Write what is left here, making sure to keep them in their order.

_____   _____

_____   _____

_____   _____

2. Cross out any repeated letters; keep the first of each letter but remove any duplicates.

_____   _____

_____   _____

_____   _____

3. Convert the letters to numbers then cross out any repeated numbers. Once you assign a number to each letter, keep the first presentation of the number and remove the duplicates. It is very important to do this in order.

1	2	3	4	5	6	7	8	9
A	B	C	D	E	F	G	H	I
J	K	L	M	N	O	P	Q	R
S	T	U	V	W	X	Y	Z	

_____

Map It

Draw a large dot in the center of the first number to mark the beginning of your intent, then draw a line through every number's center point in the chart below in the order they appear in your number.

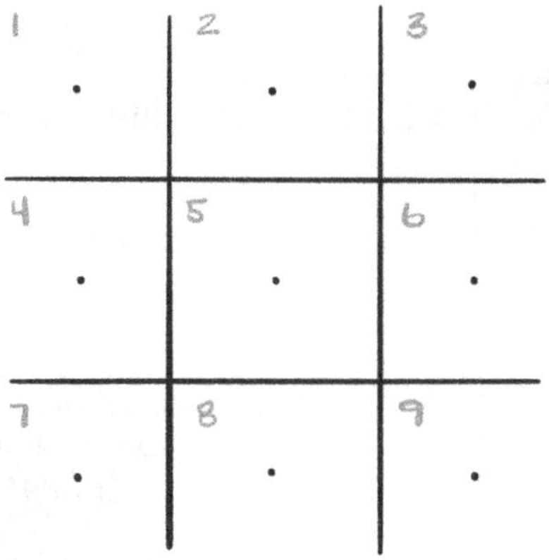

Done! Now Practice

Hone the shape into what suits you best, just make sure to do the points in order and speak your manifestation as you draw it.

Write your intention
Make a list of words that form your intention.

_____

_____

_____

Distillation (optional)
Rewrite your words with clear intentions into a short, concise sentence.

_____

_____

_____

*With thought and accuracy, think of how each word
will manifest itself as you follow these next steps.
This is action with intention. Take it slow.*

1. Cross out all of the vowels in your words/sentence. Write what is left here, making sure to keep them in their order.

_____   _____

_____   _____

_____   _____

2. Cross out any repeated letters; keep the first of each letter but remove any duplicates.

_____   _____

_____   _____

_____   _____

3. Convert the letters to numbers then cross out any repeated numbers. Once you assign a number to each letter, keep the first presentation of the number and remove the duplicates. It is very important to do this in order.

1	2	3	4	5	6	7	8	9
A	B	C	D	E	F	G	H	I
J	K	L	M	N	O	P	Q	R
S	T	U	V	W	X	Y	Z	

_____

Map It

Draw a large dot in the center of the first number to mark the beginning of your intent, then draw a line through every number's center point in the chart below in the order they appear in your number.

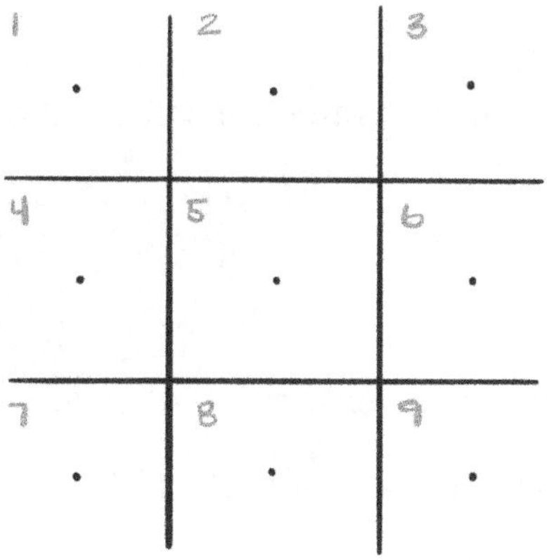

Done! Now Practice

Hone the shape into what suits you best, just make sure to do the points in order and speak your manifestation as you draw it.

Write your intention
Make a list of words that form your intention.

_____

_____

_____

Distillation (optional)
Rewrite your words with clear intentions into a short, concise sentence.

_____

_____

_____

*With thought and accuracy, think of how each word
will manifest itself as you follow these next steps.
This is action with intention. Take it slow.*

1. Cross out all of the vowels in your words/sentence. Write what is left
here, making sure to keep them in their order.

_____   _____

_____   _____

_____   _____

2. Cross out any repeated letters; keep the first of each letter but remove
any duplicates.

_____   _____

_____   _____

_____   _____

3. Convert the letters to numbers then cross out any repeated numbers.
Once you assign a number to each letter, keep the first presentation of
the number and remove the duplicates. It is very important to do this
in order.

1	2	3	4	5	6	7	8	9
A	B	C	D	E	F	G	H	I
J	K	L	M	N	O	P	Q	R
S	T	U	V	W	X	Y	Z	

_____

Map It
Draw a large dot in the center of the first number to mark the beginning of your intent, then draw a line through every number's center point in the chart below in the order they appear in your number.

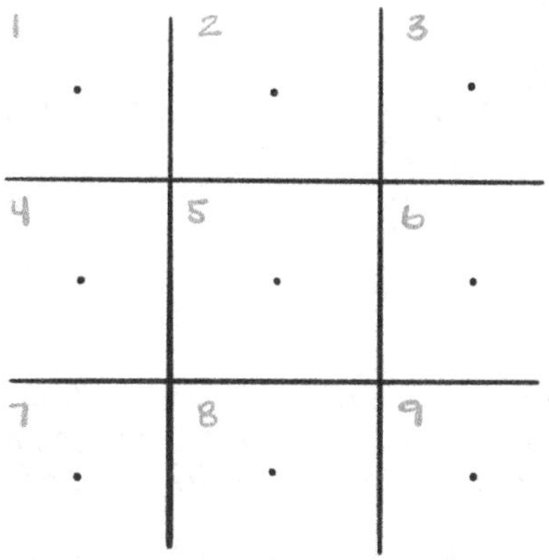

Done! Now Practice
Hone the shape into what suits you best, just make sure to do the points in order and speak your manifestation as you draw it.

Write your intention
Make a list of words that form your intention.

_____

_____

_____

Distillation (optional)
Rewrite your words with clear intentions into a short, concise sentence.

_____

_____

_____

With thought and accuracy, think of how each word
will manifest itself as you follow these next steps.
This is action with intention. Take it slow.

1. Cross out all of the vowels in your words/sentence. Write what is left here, making sure to keep them in their order.

_____   _____

_____   _____

_____   _____

2. Cross out any repeated letters; keep the first of each letter but remove any duplicates.

_____   _____

_____   _____

_____   _____

3. Convert the letters to numbers then cross out any repeated numbers. Once you assign a number to each letter, keep the first presentation of the number and remove the duplicates. It is very important to do this in order.

1	2	3	4	5	6	7	8	9
A	B	C	D	E	F	G	H	I
J	K	L	M	N	O	P	Q	R
S	T	U	V	W	X	Y	Z	

_____

Map It

Draw a large dot in the center of the first number to mark the beginning of your intent, then draw a line through every number's center point in the chart below in the order they appear in your number.

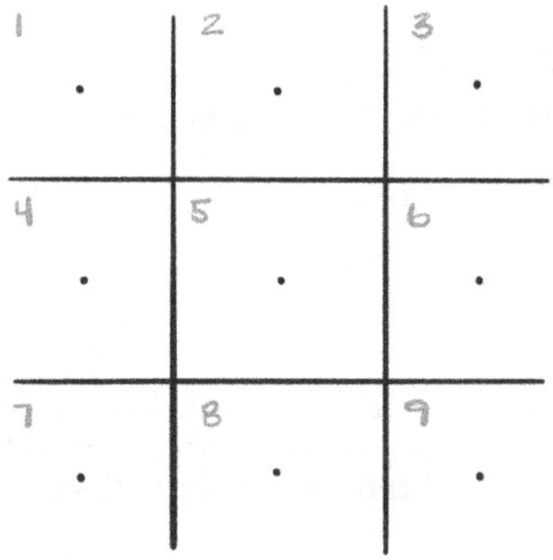

Done! Now Practice

Hone the shape into what suits you best, just make sure to do the points in order and speak your manifestation as you draw it.

Write your intention
Make a list of words that form your intention.

_____

_____

_____

Distillation (optional)
Rewrite your words with clear intentions into a short, concise sentence.

_____

_____

_____

*With thought and accuracy, think of how each word
will manifest itself as you follow these next steps.
This is action with intention. Take it slow.*

1. Cross out all of the vowels in your words/sentence. Write what is left here, making sure to keep them in their order.

_____   _____

_____   _____

_____   _____

2. Cross out any repeated letters; keep the first of each letter but remove any duplicates.

_____   _____

_____   _____

_____   _____

3. Convert the letters to numbers then cross out any repeated numbers. Once you assign a number to each letter, keep the first presentation of the number and remove the duplicates. It is very important to do this in order.

1	2	3	4	5	6	7	8	9
A	B	C	D	E	F	G	H	I
J	K	L	M	N	O	P	Q	R
S	T	U	V	W	X	Y	Z	

_____

Map It
Draw a large dot in the center of the first number to mark the beginning of your intent, then draw a line through every number's center point in the chart below in the order they appear in your number.

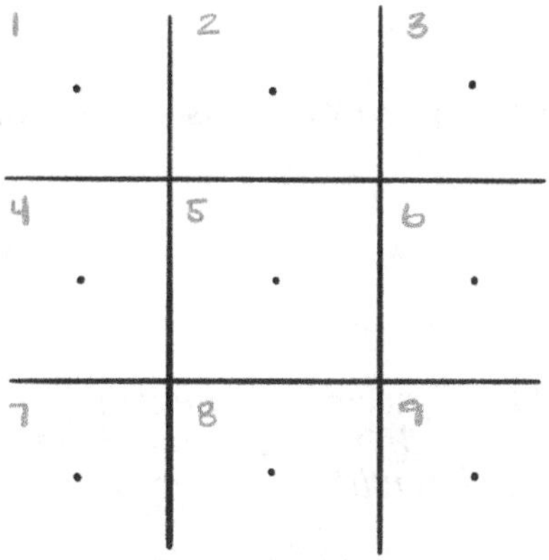

1	2	3
·	·	·
4	5	6
·	·	·
7	8	9
·	·	·

Done! Now Practice
Hone the shape into what suits you best, just make sure to do the points in order and speak your manifestation as you draw it.

Write your intention
Make a list of words that form your intention.

_____

_____

_____

Distillation (optional)
Rewrite your words with clear intentions into a short, concise sentence.

_____

_____

_____

With thought and accuracy, think of how each word
will manifest itself as you follow these next steps.
This is action with intention. Take it slow.

1. Cross out all of the vowels in your words/sentence. Write what is left here, making sure to keep them in their order.

_____   _____

_____   _____

_____   _____

2. Cross out any repeated letters; keep the first of each letter but remove any duplicates.

_____   _____

_____   _____

_____   _____

3. Convert the letters to numbers then cross out any repeated numbers. Once you assign a number to each letter, keep the first presentation of the number and remove the duplicates. It is very important to do this in order.

1	2	3	4	5	6	7	8	9
A	B	C	D	E	F	G	H	I
J	K	L	M	N	O	P	Q	R
S	T	U	V	W	X	Y	Z	

_____

Map It

Draw a large dot in the center of the first number to mark the beginning of your intent, then draw a line through every number's center point in the chart below in the order they appear in your number.

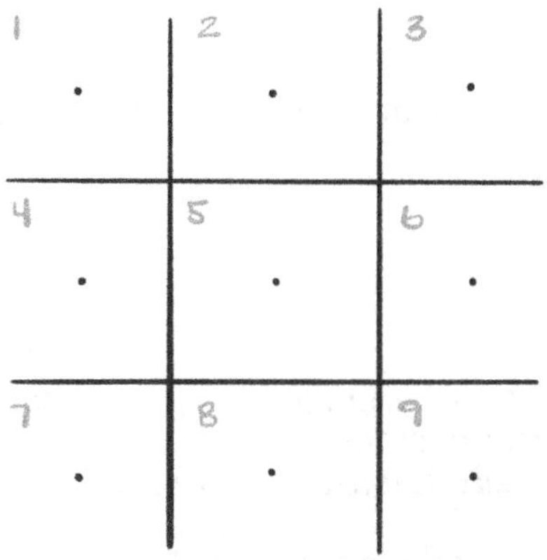

Done! Now Practice

Hone the shape into what suits you best, just make sure to do the points in order and speak your manifestation as you draw it.

Write your intention

Make a list of words that form your intention.

_____

_____

_____

Distillation (optional)

Rewrite your words with clear intentions into a short, concise sentence.

_____

_____

_____

With thought and accuracy, think of how each word
will manifest itself as you follow these next steps.
This is action with intention. Take it slow.

1. Cross out all of the vowels in your words/sentence. Write what is left here, making sure to keep them in their order.

_____   _____

_____   _____

_____   _____

2. Cross out any repeated letters; keep the first of each letter but remove any duplicates.

_____   _____

_____   _____

_____   _____

3. Convert the letters to numbers then cross out any repeated numbers. Once you assign a number to each letter, keep the first presentation of the number and remove the duplicates. It is very important to do this in order.

1	2	3	4	5	6	7	8	9
A	B	C	D	E	F	G	H	I
J	K	L	M	N	O	P	Q	R
S	T	U	V	W	X	Y	Z	

_____

Map It
Draw a large dot in the center of the first number to mark the beginning of your intent, then draw a line through every number's center point in the chart below in the order they appear in your number.

1 ·	2 ·	3 ·
4 ·	5 ·	6 ·
7 ·	8 ·	9 ·

Done! Now Practice
Hone the shape into what suits you best, just make sure to do the points in order and speak your manifestation as you draw it.

Write your intention
Make a list of words that form your intention.

_____

_____

_____

Distillation (optional)
Rewrite your words with clear intentions into a short, concise sentence.

_____

_____

_____

With thought and accuracy, think of how each word
will manifest itself as you follow these next steps.
This is action with intention. Take it slow.

1. Cross out all of the vowels in your words/sentence. Write what is left here, making sure to keep them in their order.

_____   _____

_____   _____

_____   _____

2. Cross out any repeated letters; keep the first of each letter but remove any duplicates.

_____   _____

_____   _____

_____   _____

3. Convert the letters to numbers then cross out any repeated numbers. Once you assign a number to each letter, keep the first presentation of the number and remove the duplicates. It is very important to do this in order.

1	2	3	4	5	6	7	8	9
A	B	C	D	E	F	G	H	I
J	K	L	M	N	O	P	Q	R
S	T	U	V	W	X	Y	Z	

_____

Map It

Draw a large dot in the center of the first number to mark the beginning of your intent, then draw a line through every number's center point in the chart below in the order they appear in your number.

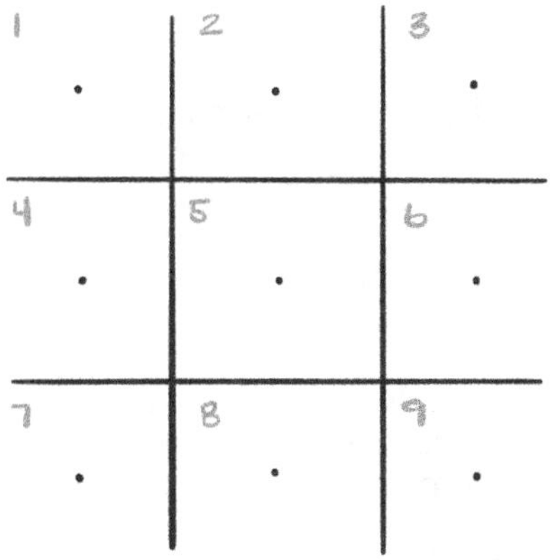

Done! Now Practice

Hone the shape into what suits you best, just make sure to do the points in order and speak your manifestation as you draw it.

Write your intention
Make a list of words that form your intention.

_____

_____

_____

Distillation (optional)
Rewrite your words with clear intentions into a short, concise sentence.

_____

_____

_____

*With thought and accuracy, think of how each word
will manifest itself as you follow these next steps.
This is action with intention. Take it slow.*

1. Cross out all of the vowels in your words/sentence. Write what is left
here, making sure to keep them in their order.

_____   _____

_____   _____

_____   _____

2. Cross out any repeated letters; keep the first of each letter but remove
any duplicates.

_____   _____

_____   _____

_____   _____

3. Convert the letters to numbers then cross out any repeated numbers.
Once you assign a number to each letter, keep the first presentation of
the number and remove the duplicates. It is very important to do this
in order.

1	2	3	4	5	6	7	8	9
A	B	C	D	E	F	G	H	I
J	K	L	M	N	O	P	Q	R
S	T	U	V	W	X	Y	Z	

_____

Map It
Draw a large dot in the center of the first number to mark the beginning of your intent, then draw a line through every number's center point in the chart below in the order they appear in your number.

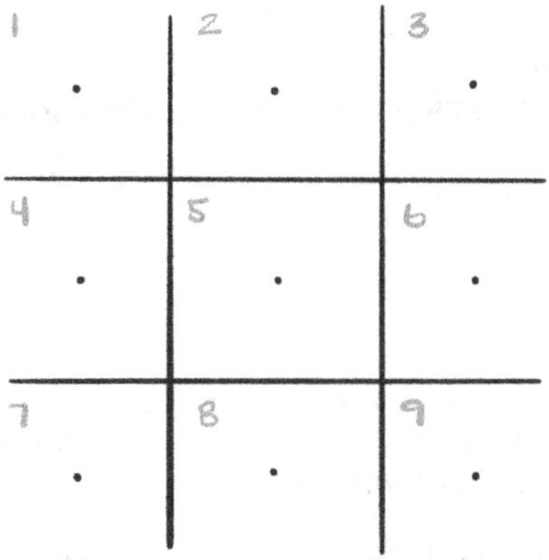

Done! Now Practice
Hone the shape into what suits you best, just make sure to do the points in order and speak your manifestation as you draw it.

Write your intention
Make a list of words that form your intention.

_____

_____

_____

Distillation (optional)
Rewrite your words with clear intentions into a short, concise sentence.

_____

_____

_____

With thought and accuracy, think of how each word
will manifest itself as you follow these next steps.
This is action with intention. Take it slow.

1. Cross out all of the vowels in your words/sentence. Write what is left here, making sure to keep them in their order.

_____   _____

_____   _____

_____   _____

2. Cross out any repeated letters; keep the first of each letter but remove any duplicates.

_____   _____

_____   _____

_____   _____

3. Convert the letters to numbers then cross out any repeated numbers. Once you assign a number to each letter, keep the first presentation of the number and remove the duplicates. It is very important to do this in order.

1	2	3	4	5	6	7	8	9
A	B	C	D	E	F	G	H	I
J	K	L	M	N	O	P	Q	R
S	T	U	V	W	X	Y	Z	

_____

Map It
Draw a large dot in the center of the first number to mark the beginning
of your intent, then draw a line through every number's center point in
the chart below in the order they appear in your number.

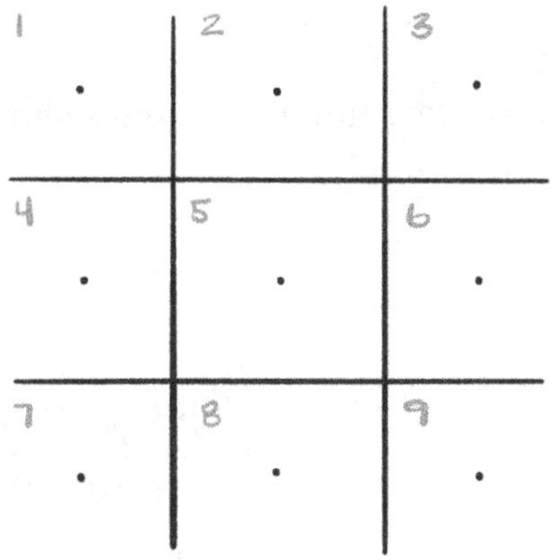

```
   1    |   2    |   3
     •  |     •  |     •
--------|--------|--------
   4    |   5    |   6
     •  |     •  |     •
--------|--------|--------
   7    |   8    |   9
     •  |     •  |     •
```

Done! Now Practice
Hone the shape into what suits you best, just make sure to do the points
in order and speak your manifestation as you draw it.

Write your intention
Make a list of words that form your intention.

_____

_____

_____

Distillation (optional)
Rewrite your words with clear intentions into a short, concise sentence.

_____

_____

_____

With thought and accuracy, think of how each word
will manifest itself as you follow these next steps.
This is action with intention. Take it slow.

1. Cross out all of the vowels in your words/sentence. Write what is left here, making sure to keep them in their order.

_____   _____

_____   _____

_____   _____

2. Cross out any repeated letters; keep the first of each letter but remove any duplicates.

_____   _____

_____   _____

_____   _____

3. Convert the letters to numbers then cross out any repeated numbers. Once you assign a number to each letter, keep the first presentation of the number and remove the duplicates. It is very important to do this in order.

1	2	3	4	5	6	7	8	9
A	B	C	D	E	F	G	H	I
J	K	L	M	N	O	P	Q	R
S	T	U	V	W	X	Y	Z	

_____

Map It

Draw a large dot in the center of the first number to mark the beginning of your intent, then draw a line through every number's center point in the chart below in the order they appear in your number.

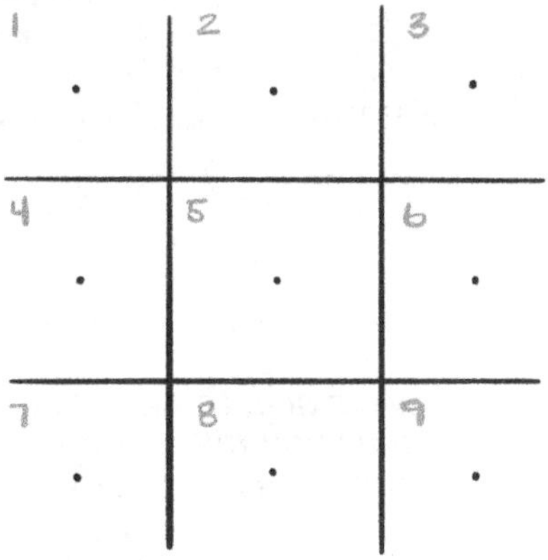

Done! Now Practice

Hone the shape into what suits you best, just make sure to do the points in order and speak your manifestation as you draw it.

Write your intention
Make a list of words that form your intention.

_____

_____

_____

Distillation (optional)
Rewrite your words with clear intentions into a short, concise sentence.

_____

_____

_____

With thought and accuracy, think of how each word
will manifest itself as you follow these next steps.
This is action with intention. Take it slow.

1. Cross out all of the vowels in your words/sentence. Write what is left here, making sure to keep them in their order.

_____   _____

_____   _____

_____   _____

2. Cross out any repeated letters; keep the first of each letter but remove any duplicates.

_____   _____

_____   _____

_____   _____

3. Convert the letters to numbers then cross out any repeated numbers. Once you assign a number to each letter, keep the first presentation of the number and remove the duplicates. It is very important to do this in order.

1	2	3	4	5	6	7	8	9
A	B	C	D	E	F	G	H	I
J	K	L	M	N	O	P	Q	R
S	T	U	V	W	X	Y	Z	

_____

Map It
Draw a large dot in the center of the first number to mark the beginning of your intent, then draw a line through every number's center point in the chart below in the order they appear in your number.

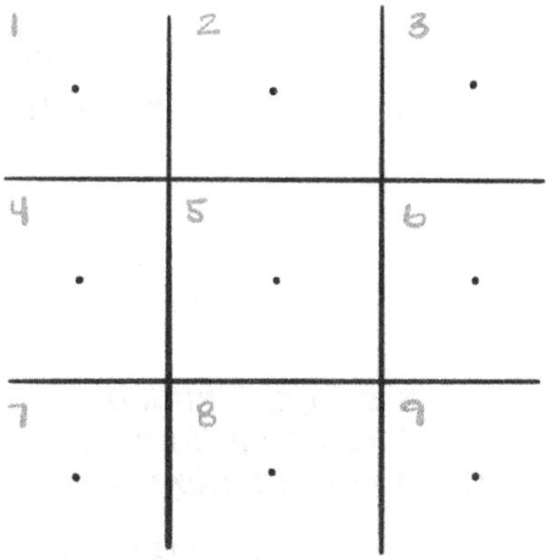

Done! Now Practice
Hone the shape into what suits you best, just make sure to do the points in order and speak your manifestation as you draw it.

Write your intention
Make a list of words that form your intention.

_____

_____

_____

Distillation (optional)
Rewrite your words with clear intentions into a short, concise sentence.

_____

_____

_____

With thought and accuracy, think of how each word
will manifest itself as you follow these next steps.
This is action with intention. Take it slow.

1. Cross out all of the vowels in your words/sentence. Write what is left here, making sure to keep them in their order.

_____   _____

_____   _____

_____   _____

2. Cross out any repeated letters; keep the first of each letter but remove any duplicates.

_____   _____

_____   _____

_____   _____

3. Convert the letters to numbers then cross out any repeated numbers. Once you assign a number to each letter, keep the first presentation of the number and remove the duplicates. It is very important to do this in order.

1	2	3	4	5	6	7	8	9
A	B	C	D	E	F	G	H	I
J	K	L	M	N	O	P	Q	R
S	T	U	V	W	X	Y	Z	

_____

Map It
Draw a large dot in the center of the first number to mark the beginning of your intent, then draw a line through every number's center point in the chart below in the order they appear in your number.

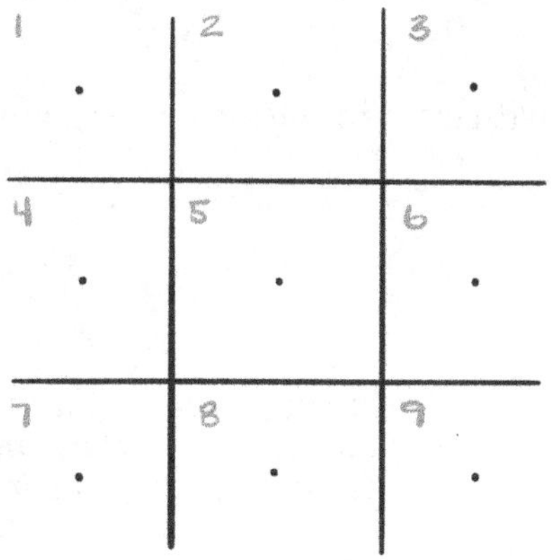

```
 1        2        3
    •        •        •

 4        5        6
    •        •        •

 7        8        9
    •        •        •
```

Done! Now Practice
Hone the shape into what suits you best, just make sure to do the points in order and speak your manifestation as you draw it.

Write your intention
Make a list of words that form your intention.

_____

_____

_____

Distillation (optional)
Rewrite your words with clear intentions into a short, concise sentence.

_____

_____

_____

*With thought and accuracy, think of how each word
will manifest itself as you follow these next steps.
This is action with intention. Take it slow.*

1. Cross out all of the vowels in your words/sentence. Write what is left here, making sure to keep them in their order.

_____   _____

_____   _____

_____   _____

2. Cross out any repeated letters; keep the first of each letter but remove any duplicates.

_____   _____

_____   _____

_____   _____

3. Convert the letters to numbers then cross out any repeated numbers. Once you assign a number to each letter, keep the first presentation of the number and remove the duplicates. It is very important to do this in order.

1	2	3	4	5	6	7	8	9
A	B	C	D	E	F	G	H	I
J	K	L	M	N	O	P	Q	R
S	T	U	V	W	X	Y	Z	

_____

Map It
Draw a large dot in the center of the first number to mark the beginning of your intent, then draw a line through every number's center point in the chart below in the order they appear in your number.

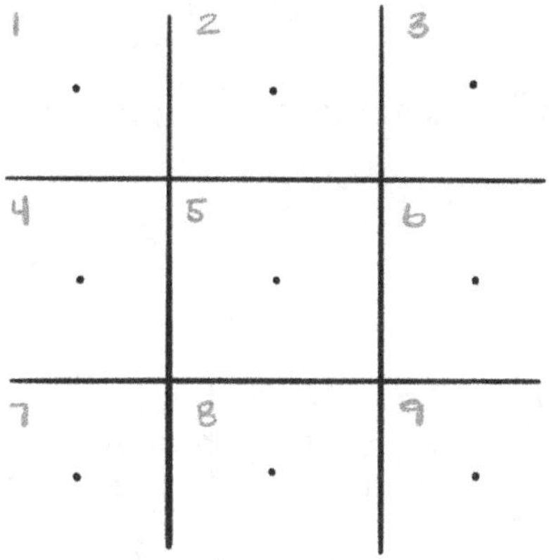

Done! Now Practice
Hone the shape into what suits you best, just make sure to do the points in order and speak your manifestation as you draw it.

Write your intention
Make a list of words that form your intention.

_____

_____

_____

Distillation (optional)
Rewrite your words with clear intentions into a short, concise sentence.

_____

_____

_____

*With thought and accuracy, think of how each word
will manifest itself as you follow these next steps.
This is action with intention. Take it slow.*

1. Cross out all of the vowels in your words/sentence. Write what is left
here, making sure to keep them in their order.

_____   _____

_____   _____

_____   _____

2. Cross out any repeated letters; keep the first of each letter but remove
any duplicates.

_____   _____

_____   _____

_____   _____

3. Convert the letters to numbers then cross out any repeated numbers.
Once you assign a number to each letter, keep the first presentation of
the number and remove the duplicates. It is very important to do this
in order.

1	2	3	4	5	6	7	8	9
A	B	C	D	E	F	G	H	I
J	K	L	M	N	O	P	Q	R
S	T	U	V	W	X	Y	Z	

_____

Map It

Draw a large dot in the center of the first number to mark the beginning of your intent, then draw a line through every number's center point in the chart below in the order they appear in your number.

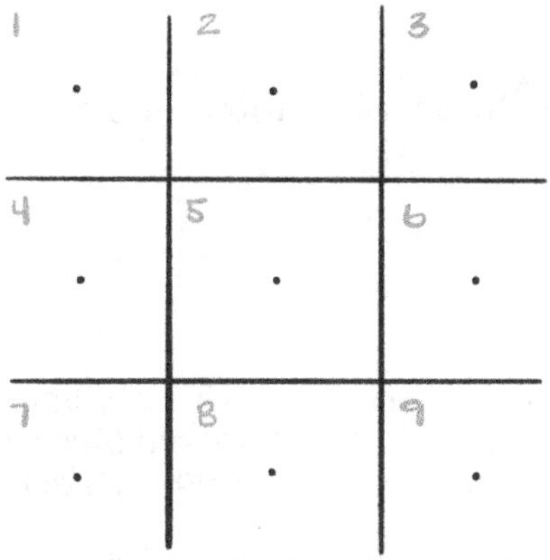

```
 1    |  2    |  3
   .  |    .  |    .
_____|_____|_____
 4    |  5    |  6
   .  |    .  |    .
_____|_____|_____
 7    |  8    |  9
   .  |    .  |    .
```

Done! Now Practice

Hone the shape into what suits you best, just make sure to do the points in order and speak your manifestation as you draw it.

Write your intention
Make a list of words that form your intention.

_____

_____

_____

Distillation (optional)
Rewrite your words with clear intentions into a short, concise sentence.

_____

_____

_____

*With thought and accuracy, think of how each word
will manifest itself as you follow these next steps.
This is action with intention. Take it slow.*

1. Cross out all of the vowels in your words/sentence. Write what is left here, making sure to keep them in their order.

_____   _____

_____   _____

_____   _____

2. Cross out any repeated letters; keep the first of each letter but remove any duplicates.

_____   _____

_____   _____

_____   _____

3. Convert the letters to numbers then cross out any repeated numbers. Once you assign a number to each letter, keep the first presentation of the number and remove the duplicates. It is very important to do this in order.

1	2	3	4	5	6	7	8	9
A	B	C	D	E	F	G	H	I
J	K	L	M	N	O	P	Q	R
S	T	U	V	W	X	Y	Z	

_____

Map It
Draw a large dot in the center of the first number to mark the beginning of your intent, then draw a line through every number's center point in the chart below in the order they appear in your number.

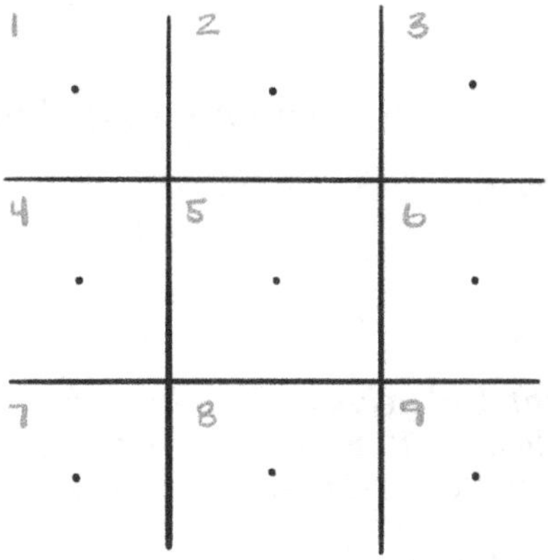

1	2	3
•	•	•
4	5	6
•	•	•
7	8	9
•	•	•

Done! Now Practice
Hone the shape into what suits you best, just make sure to do the points in order and speak your manifestation as you draw it.

Write your intention
Make a list of words that form your intention.

_____

_____

_____

Distillation (optional)
Rewrite your words with clear intentions into a short, concise sentence.

_____

_____

_____

With thought and accuracy, think of how each word
will manifest itself as you follow these next steps.
This is action with intention. Take it slow.

1. Cross out all of the vowels in your words/sentence. Write what is left here, making sure to keep them in their order.

_____   _____

_____   _____

_____   _____

2. Cross out any repeated letters; keep the first of each letter but remove any duplicates.

_____   _____

_____   _____

_____   _____

3. Convert the letters to numbers then cross out any repeated numbers. Once you assign a number to each letter, keep the first presentation of the number and remove the duplicates. It is very important to do this in order.

1	2	3	4	5	6	7	8	9
A	B	C	D	E	F	G	H	I
J	K	L	M	N	O	P	Q	R
S	T	U	V	W	X	Y	Z	

_____

Map It
Draw a large dot in the center of the first number to mark the beginning
of your intent, then draw a line through every number's center point in
the chart below in the order they appear in your number.

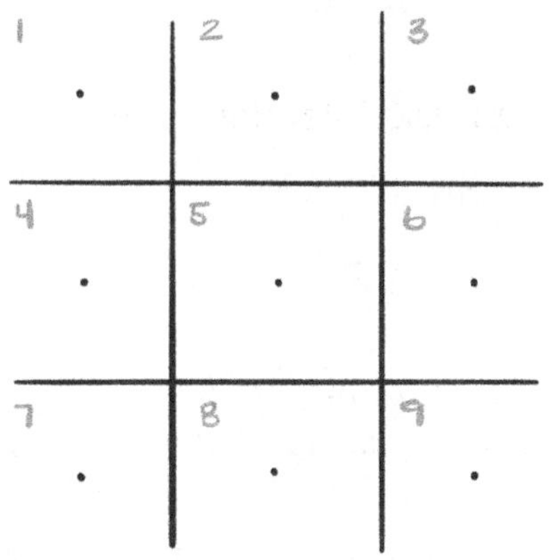

Done! Now Practice
Hone the shape into what suits you best, just make sure to do the points
in order and speak your manifestation as you draw it.

Write your intention
Make a list of words that form your intention.

_____

_____

_____

Distillation (optional)
Rewrite your words with clear intentions into a short, concise sentence.

_____

_____

_____

*With thought and accuracy, think of how each word
will manifest itself as you follow these next steps.
This is action with intention. Take it slow.*

1. Cross out all of the vowels in your words/sentence. Write what is left
here, making sure to keep them in their order.

_____   _____

_____   _____

_____   _____

2. Cross out any repeated letters; keep the first of each letter but remove
any duplicates.

_____   _____

_____   _____

_____   _____

3. Convert the letters to numbers then cross out any repeated numbers.
Once you assign a number to each letter, keep the first presentation of
the number and remove the duplicates. It is very important to do this
in order.

1	2	3	4	5	6	7	8	9
A	B	C	D	E	F	G	H	I
J	K	L	M	N	O	P	Q	R
S	T	U	V	W	X	Y	Z	

_____

Map It

Draw a large dot in the center of the first number to mark the beginning of your intent, then draw a line through every number's center point in the chart below in the order they appear in your number.

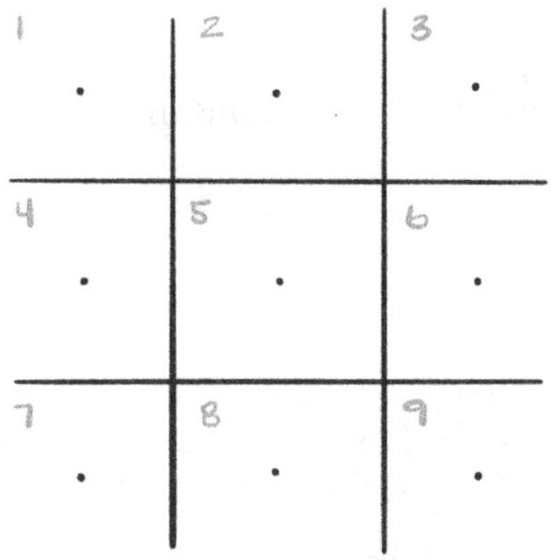

Done! Now Practice

Hone the shape into what suits you best, just make sure to do the points in order and speak your manifestation as you draw it.

Write your intention
Make a list of words that form your intention.

_____

_____

_____

Distillation (optional)
Rewrite your words with clear intentions into a short, concise sentence.

_____

_____

_____

*With thought and accuracy, think of how each word
will manifest itself as you follow these next steps.
This is action with intention. Take it slow.*

1. Cross out all of the vowels in your words/sentence. Write what is left here, making sure to keep them in their order.

_____   _____

_____   _____

_____   _____

2. Cross out any repeated letters; keep the first of each letter but remove any duplicates.

_____   _____

_____   _____

_____   _____

3. Convert the letters to numbers then cross out any repeated numbers. Once you assign a number to each letter, keep the first presentation of the number and remove the duplicates. It is very important to do this in order.

1	2	3	4	5	6	7	8	9
A	B	C	D	E	F	G	H	I
J	K	L	M	N	O	P	Q	R
S	T	U	V	W	X	Y	Z	

_____

Map It
Draw a large dot in the center of the first number to mark the beginning of your intent, then draw a line through every number's center point in the chart below in the order they appear in your number.

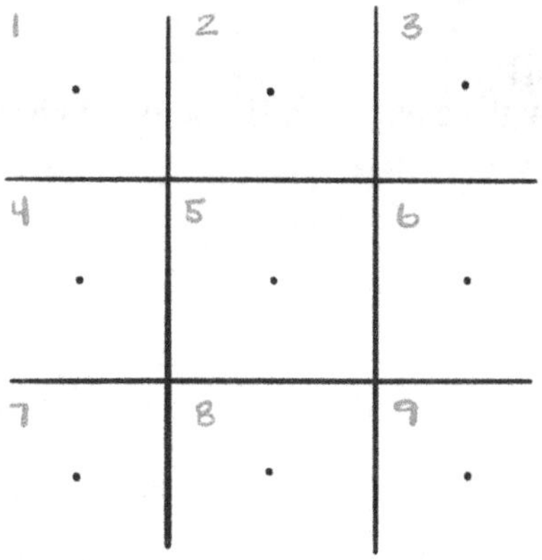

1	2	3
·	·	·
4	5	6
·	·	·
7	8	9
·	·	·

Done! Now Practice
Hone the shape into what suits you best, just make sure to do the points in order and speak your manifestation as you draw it.

Write your intention
Make a list of words that form your intention.

_____

_____

_____

Distillation (optional)
Rewrite your words with clear intentions into a short, concise sentence.

_____

_____

_____

With thought and accuracy, think of how each word
will manifest itself as you follow these next steps.
This is action with intention. Take it slow.

1. Cross out all of the vowels in your words/sentence. Write what is left here, making sure to keep them in their order.

_____   _____

_____   _____

_____   _____

2. Cross out any repeated letters; keep the first of each letter but remove any duplicates.

_____   _____

_____   _____

_____   _____

3. Convert the letters to numbers then cross out any repeated numbers. Once you assign a number to each letter, keep the first presentation of the number and remove the duplicates. It is very important to do this in order.

1	2	3	4	5	6	7	8	9
A	B	C	D	E	F	G	H	I
J	K	L	M	N	O	P	Q	R
S	T	U	V	W	X	Y	Z	

_____

Map It
Draw a large dot in the center of the first number to mark the beginning of your intent, then draw a line through every number's center point in the chart below in the order they appear in your number.

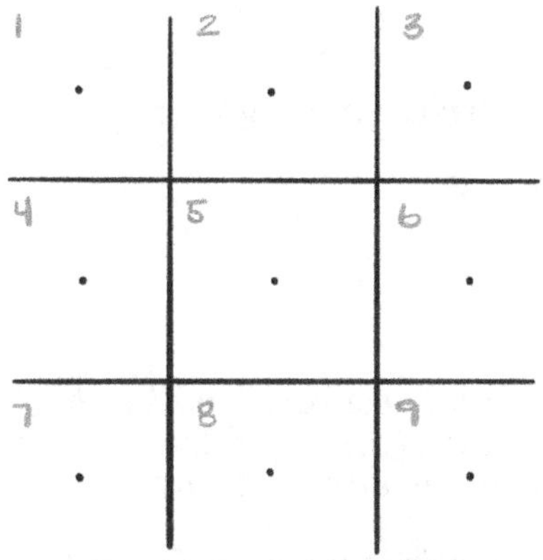

Done! Now Practice
Hone the shape into what suits you best, just make sure to do the points in order and speak your manifestation as you draw it.

Write your intention
Make a list of words that form your intention.

_____

_____

_____

Distillation (optional)
Rewrite your words with clear intentions into a short, concise sentence.

_____

_____

_____

*With thought and accuracy, think of how each word
will manifest itself as you follow these next steps.
This is action with intention. Take it slow.*

1. Cross out all of the vowels in your words/sentence. Write what is left here, making sure to keep them in their order.

_____   _____

_____   _____

_____   _____

2. Cross out any repeated letters; keep the first of each letter but remove any duplicates.

_____   _____

_____   _____

_____   _____

3. Convert the letters to numbers then cross out any repeated numbers. Once you assign a number to each letter, keep the first presentation of the number and remove the duplicates. It is very important to do this in order.

1	2	3	4	5	6	7	8	9
A	B	C	D	E	F	G	H	I
J	K	L	M	N	O	P	Q	R
S	T	U	V	W	X	Y	Z	

_____

Map It

Draw a large dot in the center of the first number to mark the beginning of your intent, then draw a line through every number's center point in the chart below in the order they appear in your number.

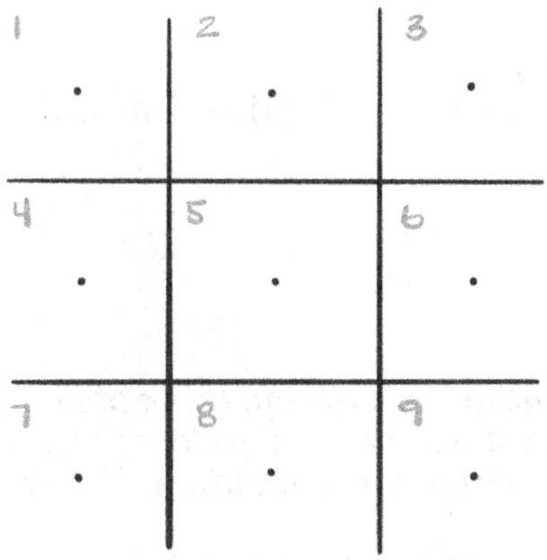

Done! Now Practice

Hone the shape into what suits you best, just make sure to do the points in order and speak your manifestation as you draw it.

Write your intention
Make a list of words that form your intention.

_____

_____

_____

Distillation (optional)
Rewrite your words with clear intentions into a short, concise sentence.

_____

_____

_____

With thought and accuracy, think of how each word
will manifest itself as you follow these next steps.
This is action with intention. Take it slow.

1. Cross out all of the vowels in your words/sentence. Write what is left here, making sure to keep them in their order.

_____   _____

_____   _____

_____   _____

2. Cross out any repeated letters; keep the first of each letter but remove any duplicates.

_____   _____

_____   _____

_____   _____

3. Convert the letters to numbers then cross out any repeated numbers. Once you assign a number to each letter, keep the first presentation of the number and remove the duplicates. It is very important to do this in order.

1	2	3	4	5	6	7	8	9
A	B	C	D	E	F	G	H	I
J	K	L	M	N	O	P	Q	R
S	T	U	V	W	X	Y	Z	

_____

Map It

Draw a large dot in the center of the first number to mark the beginning of your intent, then draw a line through every number's center point in the chart below in the order they appear in your number.

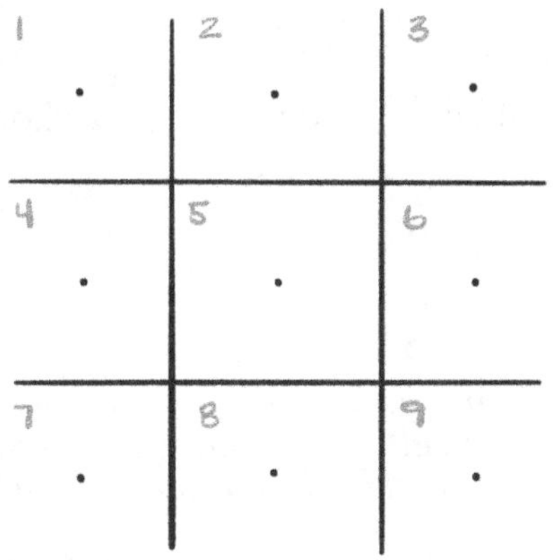

Done! Now Practice

Hone the shape into what suits you best, just make sure to do the points in order and speak your manifestation as you draw it.

Write your intention
Make a list of words that form your intention.

_____

_____

_____

Distillation (optional)
Rewrite your words with clear intentions into a short, concise sentence.

_____

_____

_____

With thought and accuracy, think of how each word
will manifest itself as you follow these next steps.
This is action with intention. Take it slow.

1. Cross out all of the vowels in your words/sentence. Write what is left here, making sure to keep them in their order.

_____   _____

_____   _____

_____   _____

2. Cross out any repeated letters; keep the first of each letter but remove any duplicates.

_____   _____

_____   _____

_____   _____

3. Convert the letters to numbers then cross out any repeated numbers. Once you assign a number to each letter, keep the first presentation of the number and remove the duplicates. It is very important to do this in order.

1	2	3	4	5	6	7	8	9
A	B	C	D	E	F	G	H	I
J	K	L	M	N	O	P	Q	R
S	T	U	V	W	X	Y	Z	

_____

Map It

Draw a large dot in the center of the first number to mark the beginning of your intent, then draw a line through every number's center point in the chart below in the order they appear in your number.

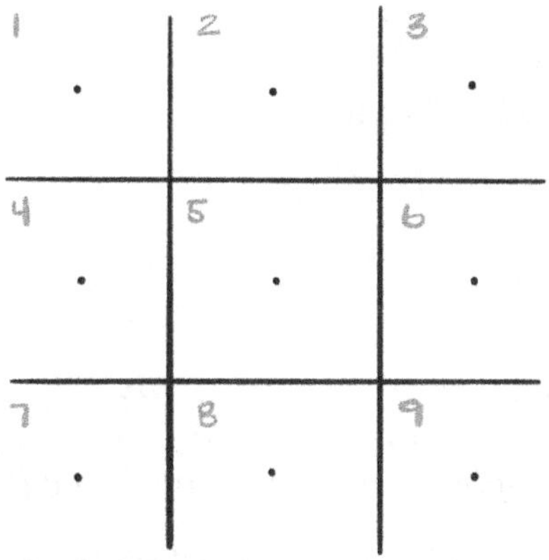

Done! Now Practice

Hone the shape into what suits you best, just make sure to do the points in order and speak your manifestation as you draw it.

Write your intention
Make a list of words that form your intention.

_____

_____

_____

Distillation (optional)
Rewrite your words with clear intentions into a short, concise sentence.

_____

_____

_____

With thought and accuracy, think of how each word
will manifest itself as you follow these next steps.
This is action with intention. Take it slow.

1. Cross out all of the vowels in your words/sentence. Write what is left here, making sure to keep them in their order.

_____   _____

_____   _____

_____   _____

2. Cross out any repeated letters; keep the first of each letter but remove any duplicates.

_____   _____

_____   _____

_____   _____

3. Convert the letters to numbers then cross out any repeated numbers. Once you assign a number to each letter, keep the first presentation of the number and remove the duplicates. It is very important to do this in order.

1	2	3	4	5	6	7	8	9
A	B	C	D	E	F	G	H	I
J	K	L	M	N	O	P	Q	R
S	T	U	V	W	X	Y	Z	

_____

Map It

Draw a large dot in the center of the first number to mark the beginning of your intent, then draw a line through every number's center point in the chart below in the order they appear in your number.

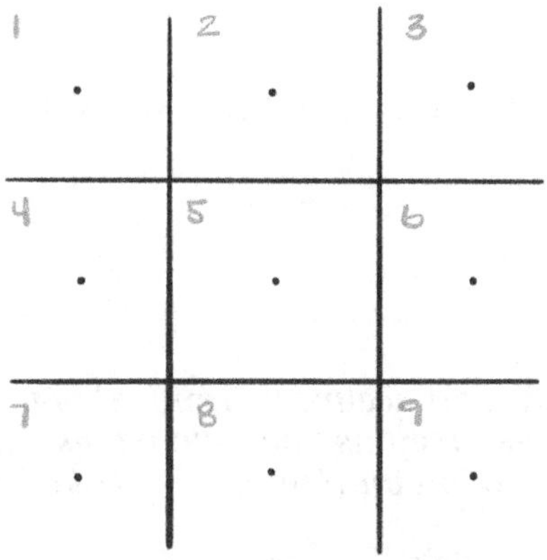

Done! Now Practice

Hone the shape into what suits you best, just make sure to do the points in order and speak your manifestation as you draw it.

Write your intention
Make a list of words that form your intention.

_____

_____

_____

Distillation (optional)
Rewrite your words with clear intentions into a short, concise sentence.

_____

_____

_____

With thought and accuracy, think of how each word
will manifest itself as you follow these next steps.
This is action with intention. Take it slow.

1. Cross out all of the vowels in your words/sentence. Write what is left here, making sure to keep them in their order.

_____   _____

_____   _____

_____   _____

2. Cross out any repeated letters; keep the first of each letter but remove any duplicates.

_____   _____

_____   _____

_____   _____

3. Convert the letters to numbers then cross out any repeated numbers. Once you assign a number to each letter, keep the first presentation of the number and remove the duplicates. It is very important to do this in order.

1	2	3	4	5	6	7	8	9
A	B	C	D	E	F	G	H	I
J	K	L	M	N	O	P	Q	R
S	T	U	V	W	X	Y	Z	

_____

Map It

Draw a large dot in the center of the first number to mark the beginning of your intent, then draw a line through every number's center point in the chart below in the order they appear in your number.

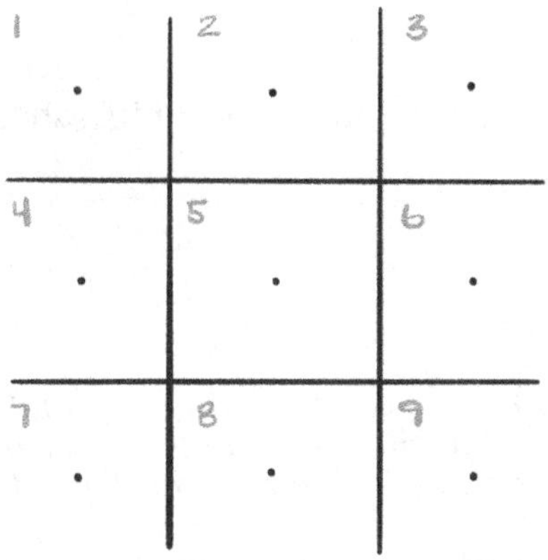

Done! Now Practice

Hone the shape into what suits you best, just make sure to do the points in order and speak your manifestation as you draw it.

Write your intention
Make a list of words that form your intention.

_____

_____

_____

Distillation (optional)
Rewrite your words with clear intentions into a short, concise sentence.

_____

_____

_____

With thought and accuracy, think of how each word
will manifest itself as you follow these next steps.
This is action with intention. Take it slow.

1. Cross out all of the vowels in your words/sentence. Write what is left
here, making sure to keep them in their order.

_____   _____

_____   _____

_____   _____

2. Cross out any repeated letters; keep the first of each letter but remove
any duplicates.

_____   _____

_____   _____

_____   _____

3. Convert the letters to numbers then cross out any repeated numbers.
Once you assign a number to each letter, keep the first presentation of
the number and remove the duplicates. It is very important to do this
in order.

1	2	3	4	5	6	7	8	9
A	B	C	D	E	F	G	H	I
J	K	L	M	N	O	P	Q	R
S	T	U	V	W	X	Y	Z	

_____

Map It
Draw a large dot in the center of the first number to mark the beginning of your intent, then draw a line through every number's center point in the chart below in the order they appear in your number.

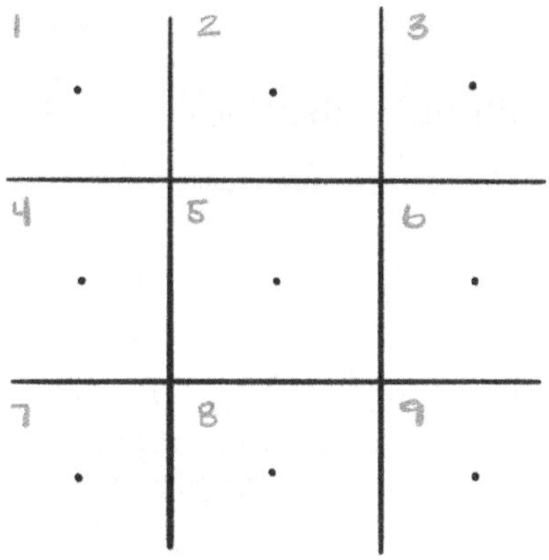

Done! Now Practice
Hone the shape into what suits you best, just make sure to do the points in order and speak your manifestation as you draw it.

Write your intention
Make a list of words that form your intention.

_____

_____

_____

Distillation (optional)
Rewrite your words with clear intentions into a short, concise sentence.

_____

_____

_____

With thought and accuracy, think of how each word
will manifest itself as you follow these next steps.
This is action with intention. Take it slow.

1. Cross out all of the vowels in your words/sentence. Write what is left here, making sure to keep them in their order.

_____   _____

_____   _____

_____   _____

2. Cross out any repeated letters; keep the first of each letter but remove any duplicates.

_____   _____

_____   _____

_____   _____

3. Convert the letters to numbers then cross out any repeated numbers. Once you assign a number to each letter, keep the first presentation of the number and remove the duplicates. It is very important to do this in order.

1	2	3	4	5	6	7	8	9
A	B	C	D	E	F	G	H	I
J	K	L	M	N	O	P	Q	R
S	T	U	V	W	X	Y	Z	

_____

Map It

Draw a large dot in the center of the first number to mark the beginning of your intent, then draw a line through every number's center point in the chart below in the order they appear in your number.

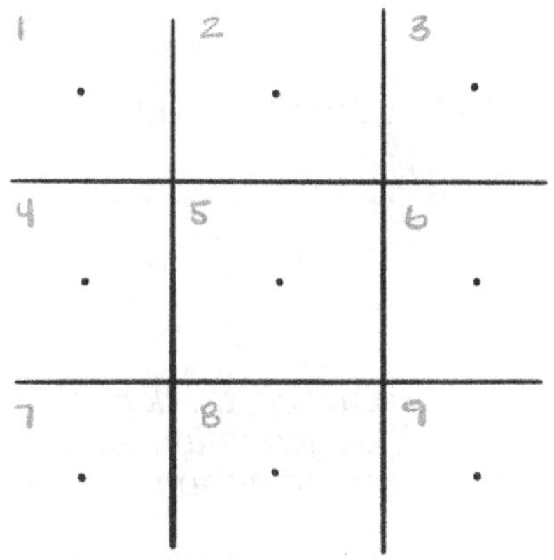

Done! Now Practice

Hone the shape into what suits you best, just make sure to do the points in order and speak your manifestation as you draw it.

Write your intention
Make a list of words that form your intention.

_____

_____

_____

Distillation (optional)
Rewrite your words with clear intentions into a short, concise sentence.

_____

_____

_____

With thought and accuracy, think of how each word
will manifest itself as you follow these next steps.
This is action with intention. Take it slow.

1. Cross out all of the vowels in your words/sentence. Write what is left here, making sure to keep them in their order.

_____   _____

_____   _____

_____   _____

2. Cross out any repeated letters; keep the first of each letter but remove any duplicates.

_____   _____

_____   _____

_____   _____

3. Convert the letters to numbers then cross out any repeated numbers. Once you assign a number to each letter, keep the first presentation of the number and remove the duplicates. It is very important to do this in order.

1	2	3	4	5	6	7	8	9
A	B	C	D	E	F	G	H	I
J	K	L	M	N	O	P	Q	R
S	T	U	V	W	X	Y	Z	

_____

Map It

Draw a large dot in the center of the first number to mark the beginning of your intent, then draw a line through every number's center point in the chart below in the order they appear in your number.

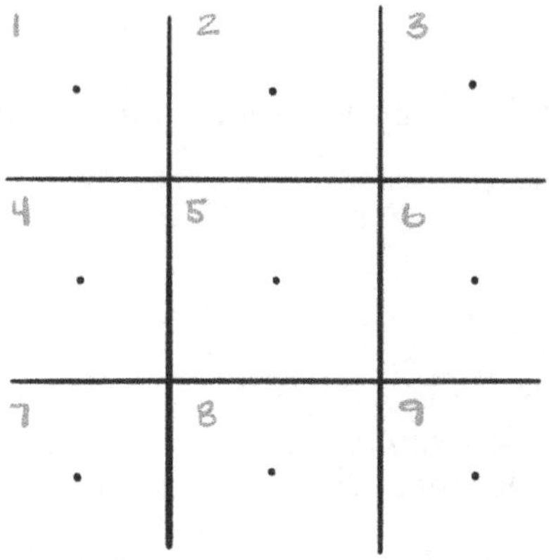

Done! Now Practice

Hone the shape into what suits you best, just make sure to do the points in order and speak your manifestation as you draw it.

Write your intention
Make a list of words that form your intention.

_____

_____

_____

Distillation (optional)
Rewrite your words with clear intentions into a short, concise sentence.

_____

_____

_____

With thought and accuracy, think of how each word
will manifest itself as you follow these next steps.
This is action with intention. Take it slow.

1. Cross out all of the vowels in your words/sentence. Write what is left here, making sure to keep them in their order.

_____   _____

_____   _____

_____   _____

2. Cross out any repeated letters; keep the first of each letter but remove any duplicates.

_____   _____

_____   _____

_____   _____

3. Convert the letters to numbers then cross out any repeated numbers. Once you assign a number to each letter, keep the first presentation of the number and remove the duplicates. It is very important to do this in order.

1	2	3	4	5	6	7	8	9
A	B	C	D	E	F	G	H	I
J	K	L	M	N	O	P	Q	R
S	T	U	V	W	X	Y	Z	

_____

Map It

Draw a large dot in the center of the first number to mark the beginning of your intent, then draw a line through every number's center point in the chart below in the order they appear in your number.

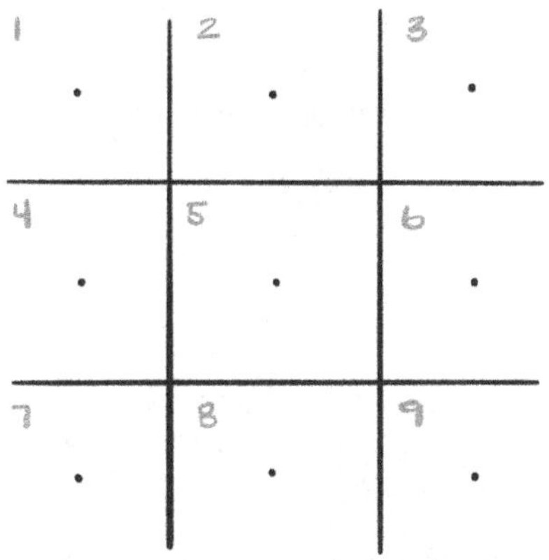

Done! Now Practice

Hone the shape into what suits you best, just make sure to do the points in order and speak your manifestation as you draw it.

Write your intention
Make a list of words that form your intention.

_____

_____

_____

Distillation (optional)
Rewrite your words with clear intentions into a short, concise sentence.

_____

_____

_____

With thought and accuracy, think of how each word
will manifest itself as you follow these next steps.
This is action with intention. Take it slow.

1. Cross out all of the vowels in your words/sentence. Write what is left here, making sure to keep them in their order.

_____   _____

_____   _____

_____   _____

2. Cross out any repeated letters; keep the first of each letter but remove any duplicates.

_____   _____

_____   _____

_____   _____

3. Convert the letters to numbers then cross out any repeated numbers. Once you assign a number to each letter, keep the first presentation of the number and remove the duplicates. It is very important to do this in order.

1	2	3	4	5	6	7	8	9
A	B	C	D	E	F	G	H	I
J	K	L	M	N	O	P	Q	R
S	T	U	V	W	X	Y	Z	

_____

Map It
Draw a large dot in the center of the first number to mark the beginning of your intent, then draw a line through every number's center point in the chart below in the order they appear in your number.

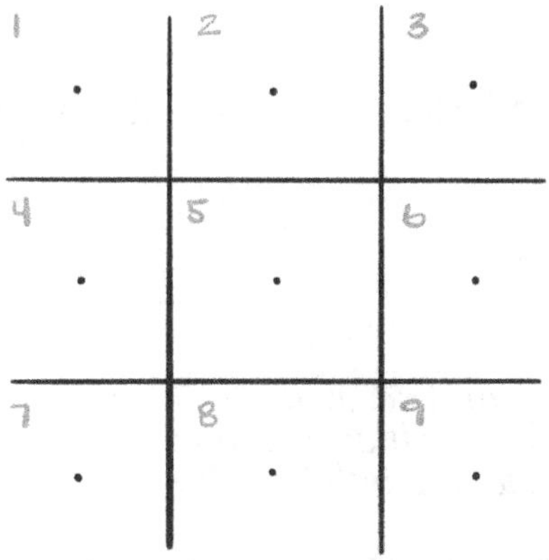

Done! Now Practice
Hone the shape into what suits you best, just make sure to do the points in order and speak your manifestation as you draw it.

Write your intention
Make a list of words that form your intention.

_____

_____

_____

Distillation (optional)
Rewrite your words with clear intentions into a short, concise sentence.

_____

_____

_____

*With thought and accuracy, think of how each word
will manifest itself as you follow these next steps.
This is action with intention. Take it slow.*

1. Cross out all of the vowels in your words/sentence. Write what is left here, making sure to keep them in their order.

_____   _____

_____   _____

_____   _____

2. Cross out any repeated letters; keep the first of each letter but remove any duplicates.

_____   _____

_____   _____

_____   _____

3. Convert the letters to numbers then cross out any repeated numbers. Once you assign a number to each letter, keep the first presentation of the number and remove the duplicates. It is very important to do this in order.

1	2	3	4	5	6	7	8	9
A	B	C	D	E	F	G	H	I
J	K	L	M	N	O	P	Q	R
S	T	U	V	W	X	Y	Z	

_____

Map It
Draw a large dot in the center of the first number to mark the beginning of your intent, then draw a line through every number's center point in the chart below in the order they appear in your number.

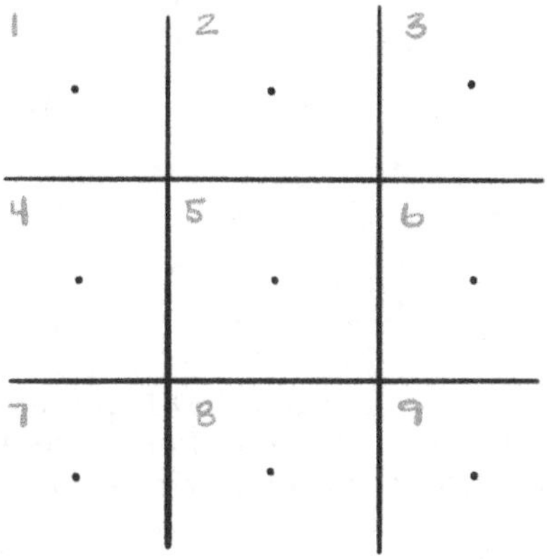

Done! Now Practice
Hone the shape into what suits you best, just make sure to do the points in order and speak your manifestation as you draw it.

Write your intention
Make a list of words that form your intention.

_____

_____

_____

Distillation (optional)
Rewrite your words with clear intentions into a short, concise sentence.

_____

_____

_____

*With thought and accuracy, think of how each word
will manifest itself as you follow these next steps.
This is action with intention. Take it slow.*

1. Cross out all of the vowels in your words/sentence. Write what is left
here, making sure to keep them in their order.

_____   _____

_____   _____

_____   _____

2. Cross out any repeated letters; keep the first of each letter but remove
any duplicates.

_____   _____

_____   _____

_____   _____

3. Convert the letters to numbers then cross out any repeated numbers.
Once you assign a number to each letter, keep the first presentation of
the number and remove the duplicates. It is very important to do this
in order.

1	2	3	4	5	6	7	8	9
A	B	C	D	E	F	G	H	I
J	K	L	M	N	O	P	Q	R
S	T	U	V	W	X	Y	Z	

_____

Map It
Draw a large dot in the center of the first number to mark the beginning of your intent, then draw a line through every number's center point in the chart below in the order they appear in your number.

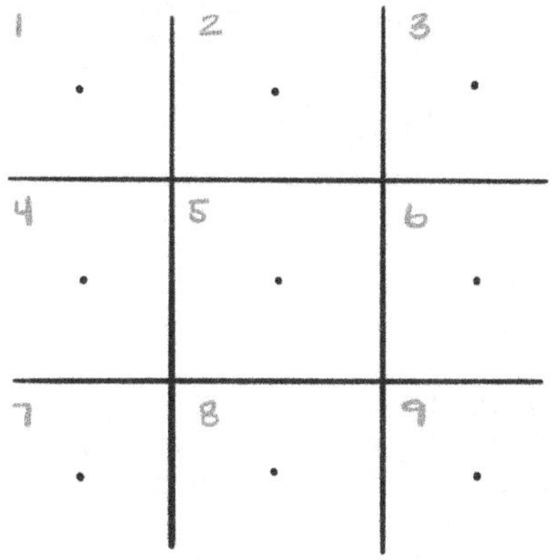

Done! Now Practice
Hone the shape into what suits you best, just make sure to do the points in order and speak your manifestation as you draw it.

Write your intention
Make a list of words that form your intention.

_____

_____

_____

Distillation (optional)
Rewrite your words with clear intentions into a short, concise sentence.

_____

_____

_____

*With thought and accuracy, think of how each word
will manifest itself as you follow these next steps.
This is action with intention. Take it slow.*

1. Cross out all of the vowels in your words/sentence. Write what is left here, making sure to keep them in their order.

_____   _____

_____   _____

_____   _____

2. Cross out any repeated letters; keep the first of each letter but remove any duplicates.

_____   _____

_____   _____

_____   _____

3. Convert the letters to numbers then cross out any repeated numbers. Once you assign a number to each letter, keep the first presentation of the number and remove the duplicates. It is very important to do this in order.

1	2	3	4	5	6	7	8	9
A	B	C	D	E	F	G	H	I
J	K	L	M	N	O	P	Q	R
S	T	U	V	W	X	Y	Z	

Map It
Draw a large dot in the center of the first number to mark the beginning
of your intent, then draw a line through every number's center point in
the chart below in the order they appear in your number.

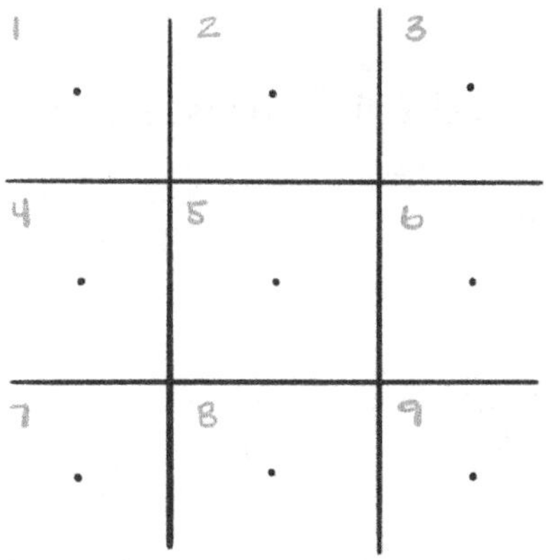

1	2	3
.	.	.
4	5	6
.	.	.
7	8	9
.	.	.

Done! Now Practice
Hone the shape into what suits you best, just make sure to do the points
in order and speak your manifestation as you draw it.

Write your intention
Make a list of words that form your intention.

_____

_____

_____

Distillation (optional)
Rewrite your words with clear intentions into a short, concise sentence.

_____

_____

_____

*With thought and accuracy, think of how each word
will manifest itself as you follow these next steps.
This is action with intention. Take it slow.*

1. Cross out all of the vowels in your words/sentence. Write what is left here, making sure to keep them in their order.

_____   _____

_____   _____

_____   _____

2. Cross out any repeated letters; keep the first of each letter but remove any duplicates.

_____   _____

_____   _____

_____   _____

3. Convert the letters to numbers then cross out any repeated numbers. Once you assign a number to each letter, keep the first presentation of the number and remove the duplicates. It is very important to do this in order.

1	2	3	4	5	6	7	8	9
A	B	C	D	E	F	G	H	I
J	K	L	M	N	O	P	Q	R
S	T	U	V	W	X	Y	Z	

_____

Map It
Draw a large dot in the center of the first number to mark the beginning
of your intent, then draw a line through every number's center point in
the chart below in the order they appear in your number.

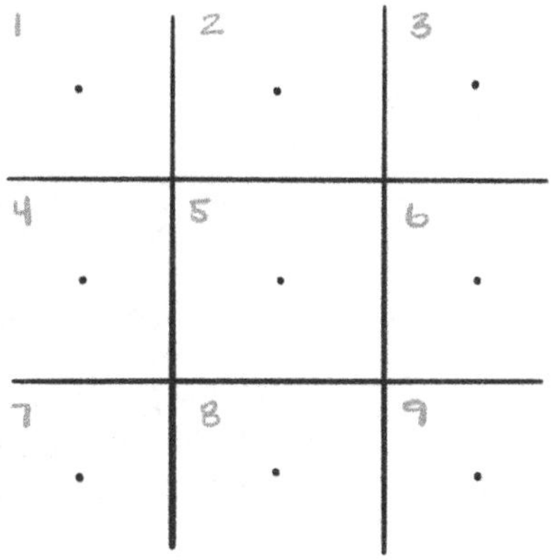

1	2	3
.	.	.
4	5	6
.	.	.
7	8	9
.	.	.

Done! Now Practice
Hone the shape into what suits you best, just make sure to do the points
in order and speak your manifestation as you draw it.

Write your intention
Make a list of words that form your intention.

_____

_____

_____

Distillation (optional)
Rewrite your words with clear intentions into a short, concise sentence.

_____

_____

_____

With thought and accuracy, think of how each word
will manifest itself as you follow these next steps.
This is action with intention. Take it slow.

1. Cross out all of the vowels in your words/sentence. Write what is left here, making sure to keep them in their order.

_____   _____

_____   _____

_____   _____

2. Cross out any repeated letters; keep the first of each letter but remove any duplicates.

_____   _____

_____   _____

_____   _____

3. Convert the letters to numbers then cross out any repeated numbers. Once you assign a number to each letter, keep the first presentation of the number and remove the duplicates. It is very important to do this in order.

1	2	3	4	5	6	7	8	9
A	B	C	D	E	F	G	H	I
J	K	L	M	N	O	P	Q	R
S	T	U	V	W	X	Y	Z	

_____

Map It

Draw a large dot in the center of the first number to mark the beginning of your intent, then draw a line through every number's center point in the chart below in the order they appear in your number.

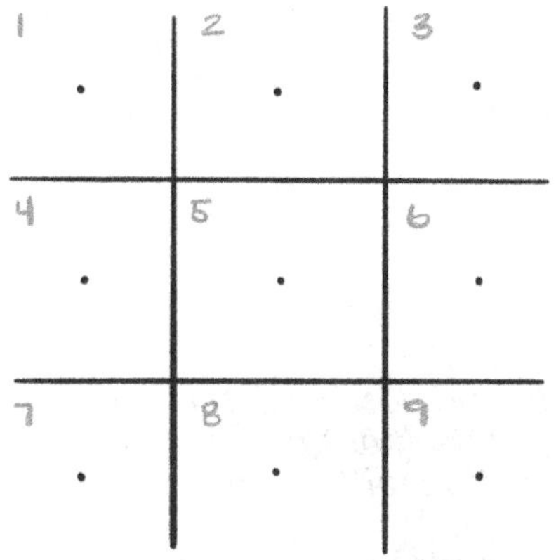

Done! Now Practice

Hone the shape into what suits you best, just make sure to do the points in order and speak your manifestation as you draw it.

Write your intention
Make a list of words that form your intention.

_____

_____

_____

Distillation (optional)
Rewrite your words with clear intentions into a short, concise sentence.

_____

_____

_____

With thought and accuracy, think of how each word
will manifest itself as you follow these next steps.
This is action with intention. Take it slow.

1. Cross out all of the vowels in your words/sentence. Write what is left here, making sure to keep them in their order.

_____   _____

_____   _____

_____   _____

2. Cross out any repeated letters; keep the first of each letter but remove any duplicates.

_____   _____

_____   _____

_____   _____

3. Convert the letters to numbers then cross out any repeated numbers. Once you assign a number to each letter, keep the first presentation of the number and remove the duplicates. It is very important to do this in order.

1	2	3	4	5	6	7	8	9
A	B	C	D	E	F	G	H	I
J	K	L	M	N	O	P	Q	R
S	T	U	V	W	X	Y	Z	

_____

Map It

Draw a large dot in the center of the first number to mark the beginning of your intent, then draw a line through every number's center point in the chart below in the order they appear in your number.

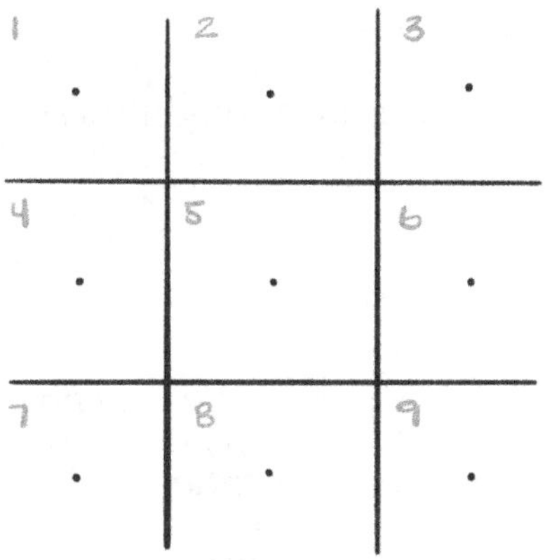

Done! Now Practice

Hone the shape into what suits you best, just make sure to do the points in order and speak your manifestation as you draw it.

Write your intention
Make a list of words that form your intention.

_____

_____

_____

Distillation (optional)
Rewrite your words with clear intentions into a short, concise sentence.

_____

_____

_____

With thought and accuracy, think of how each word
will manifest itself as you follow these next steps.
This is action with intention. Take it slow.

1. Cross out all of the vowels in your words/sentence. Write what is left here, making sure to keep them in their order.

_____   _____

_____   _____

_____   _____

2. Cross out any repeated letters; keep the first of each letter but remove any duplicates.

_____   _____

_____   _____

_____   _____

3. Convert the letters to numbers then cross out any repeated numbers. Once you assign a number to each letter, keep the first presentation of the number and remove the duplicates. It is very important to do this in order.

1	2	3	4	5	6	7	8	9
A	B	C	D	E	F	G	H	I
J	K	L	M	N	O	P	Q	R
S	T	U	V	W	X	Y	Z	

_____

Map It
Draw a large dot in the center of the first number to mark the beginning of your intent, then draw a line through every number's center point in the chart below in the order they appear in your number.

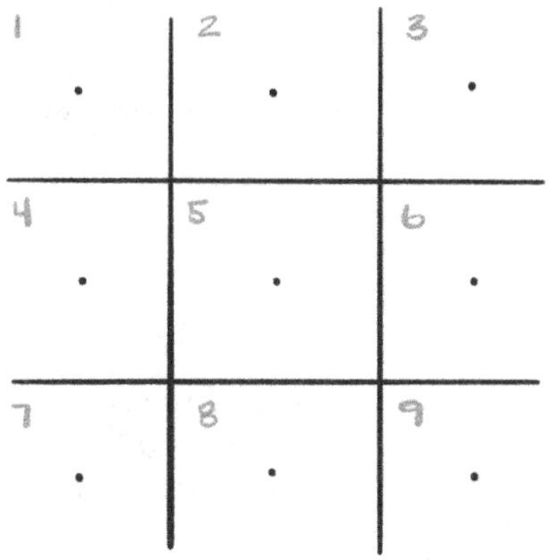

Done! Now Practice
Hone the shape into what suits you best, just make sure to do the points in order and speak your manifestation as you draw it.

Write your intention
Make a list of words that form your intention.

Distillation (optional)
Rewrite your words with clear intentions into a short, concise sentence.

---

*With thought and accuracy, think of how each word
will manifest itself as you follow these next steps.
This is action with intention. Take it slow.*

1. Cross out all of the vowels in your words/sentence. Write what is left
here, making sure to keep them in their order.

---

2. Cross out any repeated letters; keep the first of each letter but remove
any duplicates.

---

3. Convert the letters to numbers then cross out any repeated numbers.
Once you assign a number to each letter, keep the first presentation of
the number and remove the duplicates. It is very important to do this
in order.

1	2	3	4	5	6	7	8	9
A	B	C	D	E	F	G	H	I
J	K	L	M	N	O	P	Q	R
S	T	U	V	W	X	Y	Z	

Map It

Draw a large dot in the center of the first number to mark the beginning of your intent, then draw a line through every number's center point in the chart below in the order they appear in your number.

1	2	3
.	.	.
4	5	6
.	.	.
7	8	9
.	.	.

Done! Now Practice

Hone the shape into what suits you best, just make sure to do the points in order and speak your manifestation as you draw it.

Write your intention
Make a list of words that form your intention.

_____

_____

_____

Distillation (optional)
Rewrite your words with clear intentions into a short, concise sentence.

_____

_____

_____

With thought and accuracy, think of how each word
will manifest itself as you follow these next steps.
This is action with intention. Take it slow.

1. Cross out all of the vowels in your words/sentence. Write what is left here, making sure to keep them in their order.

_____   _____

_____   _____

2. Cross out any repeated letters; keep the first of each letter but remove any duplicates.

_____   _____

_____   _____

_____   _____

3. Convert the letters to numbers then cross out any repeated numbers. Once you assign a number to each letter, keep the first presentation of the number and remove the duplicates. It is very important to do this in order.

1	2	3	4	5	6	7	8	9
A	B	C	D	E	F	G	H	I
J	K	L	M	N	O	P	Q	R
S	T	U	V	W	X	Y	Z	

_____

Map It
Draw a large dot in the center of the first number to mark the beginning
of your intent, then draw a line through every number's center point in
the chart below in the order they appear in your number.

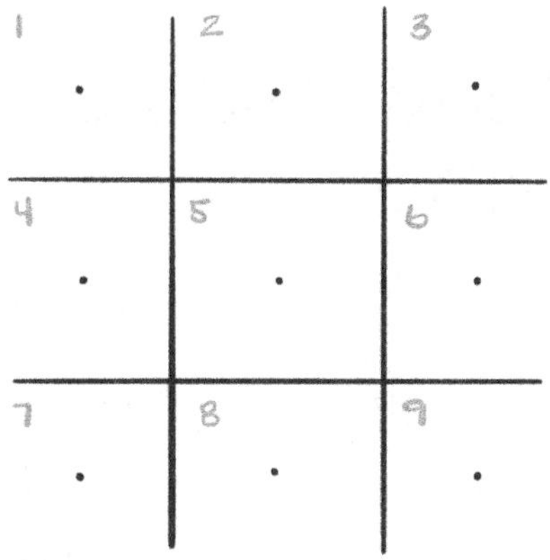

Done! Now Practice
Hone the shape into what suits you best, just make sure to do the points
in order and speak your manifestation as you draw it.

Write your intention
Make a list of words that form your intention.

_____

_____

_____

Distillation (optional)
Rewrite your words with clear intentions into a short, concise sentence.

_____

_____

_____

With thought and accuracy, think of how each word
will manifest itself as you follow these next steps.
This is action with intention. Take it slow.

1. Cross out all of the vowels in your words/sentence. Write what is left here, making sure to keep them in their order.

_____   _____

_____   _____

_____   _____

2. Cross out any repeated letters; keep the first of each letter but remove any duplicates.

_____   _____

_____   _____

_____   _____

3. Convert the letters to numbers then cross out any repeated numbers. Once you assign a number to each letter, keep the first presentation of the number and remove the duplicates. It is very important to do this in order.

1	2	3	4	5	6	7	8	9
A	B	C	D	E	F	G	H	I
J	K	L	M	N	O	P	Q	R
S	T	U	V	W	X	Y	Z	

_____

Map It

Draw a large dot in the center of the first number to mark the beginning of your intent, then draw a line through every number's center point in the chart below in the order they appear in your number.

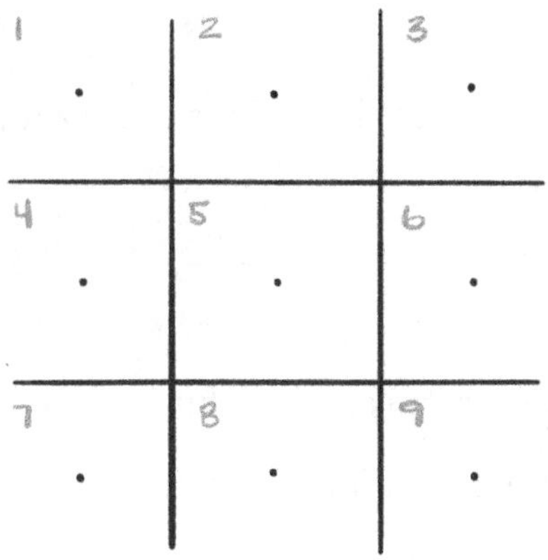

Done! Now Practice

Hone the shape into what suits you best, just make sure to do the points in order and speak your manifestation as you draw it.

Write your intention
Make a list of words that form your intention.

_____

_____

_____

Distillation (optional)
Rewrite your words with clear intentions into a short, concise sentence.

_____

_____

_____

With thought and accuracy, think of how each word
will manifest itself as you follow these next steps.
This is action with intention. Take it slow.

1. Cross out all of the vowels in your words/sentence. Write what is left here, making sure to keep them in their order.

_____   _____

_____   _____

_____   _____

2. Cross out any repeated letters; keep the first of each letter but remove any duplicates.

_____   _____

_____   _____

_____   _____

3. Convert the letters to numbers then cross out any repeated numbers. Once you assign a number to each letter, keep the first presentation of the number and remove the duplicates. It is very important to do this in order.

1	2	3	4	5	6	7	8	9
A	B	C	D	E	F	G	H	I
J	K	L	M	N	O	P	Q	R
S	T	U	V	W	X	Y	Z	

_____

Map It

Draw a large dot in the center of the first number to mark the beginning of your intent, then draw a line through every number's center point in the chart below in the order they appear in your number.

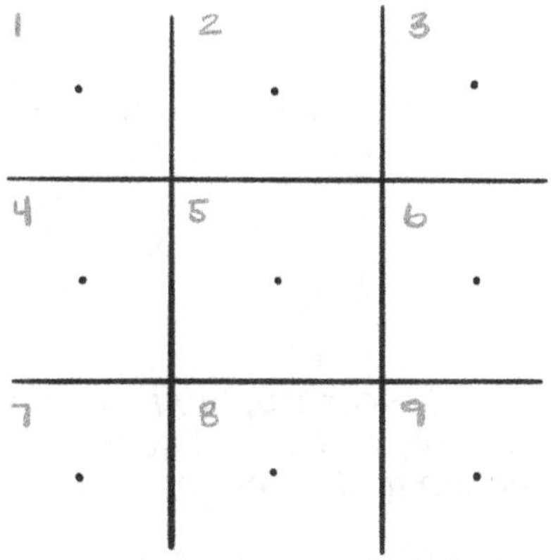

Done! Now Practice

Hone the shape into what suits you best, just make sure to do the points in order and speak your manifestation as you draw it.

Write your intention
Make a list of words that form your intention.

_____

_____

_____

Distillation (optional)
Rewrite your words with clear intentions into a short, concise sentence.

_____

_____

_____

*With thought and accuracy, think of how each word
will manifest itself as you follow these next steps.
This is action with intention. Take it slow.*

1. Cross out all of the vowels in your words/sentence. Write what is left
here, making sure to keep them in their order.

_____   _____

_____   _____

_____   _____

2. Cross out any repeated letters; keep the first of each letter but remove
any duplicates.

_____   _____

_____   _____

_____   _____

3. Convert the letters to numbers then cross out any repeated numbers.
Once you assign a number to each letter, keep the first presentation of
the number and remove the duplicates. It is very important to do this
in order.

1	2	3	4	5	6	7	8	9
A	B	C	D	E	F	G	H	I
J	K	L	M	N	O	P	Q	R
S	T	U	V	W	X	Y	Z	

_____

Map It
Draw a large dot in the center of the first number to mark the beginning
of your intent, then draw a line through every number's center point in
the chart below in the order they appear in your number.

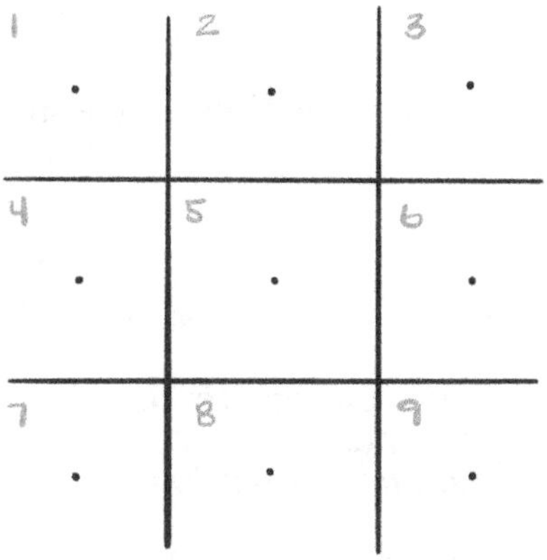

Done! Now Practice
Hone the shape into what suits you best, just make sure to do the points
in order and speak your manifestation as you draw it.

Write your intention
Make a list of words that form your intention.

_____

_____

_____

Distillation (optional)
Rewrite your words with clear intentions into a short, concise sentence.

_____

_____

_____

With thought and accuracy, think of how each word
will manifest itself as you follow these next steps.
This is action with intention. Take it slow.

1. Cross out all of the vowels in your words/sentence. Write what is left here, making sure to keep them in their order.

_____   _____

_____   _____

_____   _____

2. Cross out any repeated letters; keep the first of each letter but remove any duplicates.

_____   _____

_____   _____

_____   _____

3. Convert the letters to numbers then cross out any repeated numbers. Once you assign a number to each letter, keep the first presentation of the number and remove the duplicates. It is very important to do this in order.

1	2	3	4	5	6	7	8	9
A	B	C	D	E	F	G	H	I
J	K	L	M	N	O	P	Q	R
S	T	U	V	W	X	Y	Z	

_____

Map It

Draw a large dot in the center of the first number to mark the beginning of your intent, then draw a line through every number's center point in the chart below in the order they appear in your number.

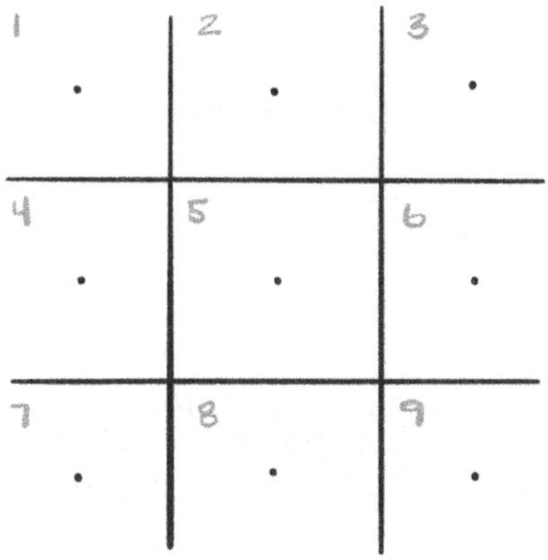

Done! Now Practice

Hone the shape into what suits you best, just make sure to do the points in order and speak your manifestation as you draw it.

Write your intention
Make a list of words that form your intention.

_____

_____

_____

Distillation (optional)
Rewrite your words with clear intentions into a short, concise sentence.

_____

_____

_____

*With thought and accuracy, think of how each word
will manifest itself as you follow these next steps.
This is action with intention. Take it slow.*

1. Cross out all of the vowels in your words/sentence. Write what is left
here, making sure to keep them in their order.

_____   _____

_____   _____

_____   _____

2. Cross out any repeated letters; keep the first of each letter but remove
any duplicates.

_____   _____

_____   _____

_____   _____

3. Convert the letters to numbers then cross out any repeated numbers.
Once you assign a number to each letter, keep the first presentation of
the number and remove the duplicates. It is very important to do this
in order.

1	2	3	4	5	6	7	8	9
A	B	C	D	E	F	G	H	I
J	K	L	M	N	O	P	Q	R
S	T	U	V	W	X	Y	Z	

_____

Map It

Draw a large dot in the center of the first number to mark the beginning of your intent, then draw a line through every number's center point in the chart below in the order they appear in your number.

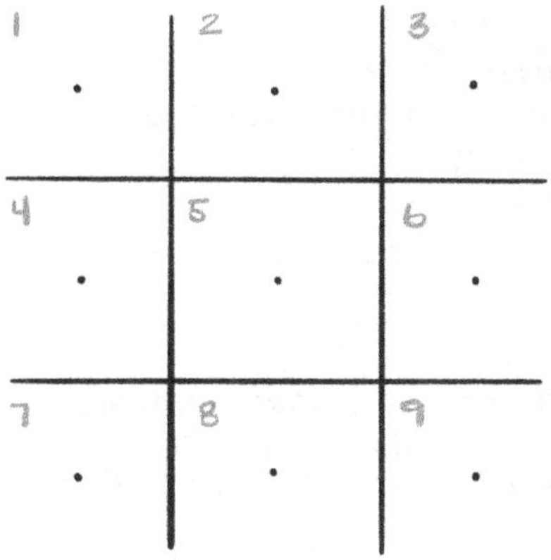

Done! Now Practice

Hone the shape into what suits you best, just make sure to do the points in order and speak your manifestation as you draw it.

Write your intention
Make a list of words that form your intention.

_____

_____

_____

Distillation (optional)
Rewrite your words with clear intentions into a short, concise sentence.

_____

_____

_____

With thought and accuracy, think of how each word
will manifest itself as you follow these next steps.
This is action with intention. Take it slow.

1. Cross out all of the vowels in your words/sentence. Write what is left here, making sure to keep them in their order.

_____   _____

_____   _____

_____   _____

2. Cross out any repeated letters; keep the first of each letter but remove any duplicates.

_____   _____

_____   _____

_____   _____

3. Convert the letters to numbers then cross out any repeated numbers. Once you assign a number to each letter, keep the first presentation of the number and remove the duplicates. It is very important to do this in order.

1	2	3	4	5	6	7	8	9
A	B	C	D	E	F	G	H	I
J	K	L	M	N	O	P	Q	R
S	T	U	V	W	X	Y	Z	

_____

Map It
Draw a large dot in the center of the first number to mark the beginning of your intent, then draw a line through every number's center point in the chart below in the order they appear in your number.

1	2	3
.	.	.
4	5	6
.	.	.
7	8	9
.	.	.

Done! Now Practice
Hone the shape into what suits you best, just make sure to do the points in order and speak your manifestation as you draw it.

Write your intention
Make a list of words that form your intention.

_____

_____

_____

Distillation (optional)
Rewrite your words with clear intentions into a short, concise sentence.

_____

_____

_____

*With thought and accuracy, think of how each word
will manifest itself as you follow these next steps.
This is action with intention. Take it slow.*

1. Cross out all of the vowels in your words/sentence. Write what is left here, making sure to keep them in their order.

_____   _____

_____   _____

_____   _____

2. Cross out any repeated letters; keep the first of each letter but remove any duplicates.

_____   _____

_____   _____

_____   _____

3. Convert the letters to numbers then cross out any repeated numbers. Once you assign a number to each letter, keep the first presentation of the number and remove the duplicates. It is very important to do this in order.

1	2	3	4	5	6	7	8	9
A	B	C	D	E	F	G	H	I
J	K	L	M	N	O	P	Q	R
S	T	U	V	W	X	Y	Z	

Map It

Draw a large dot in the center of the first number to mark the beginning of your intent, then draw a line through every number's center point in the chart below in the order they appear in your number.

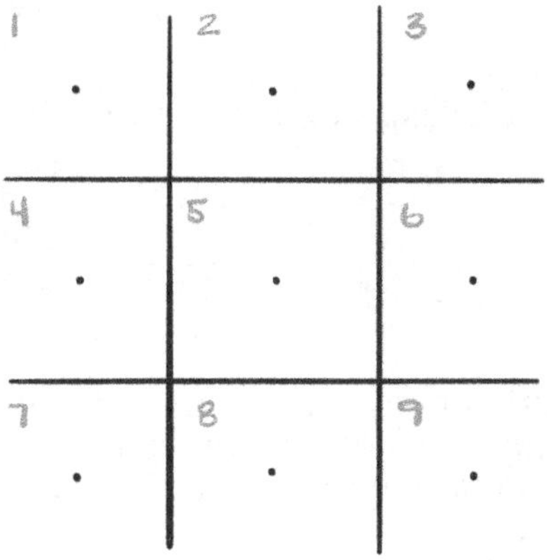

Done! Now Practice

Hone the shape into what suits you best, just make sure to do the points in order and speak your manifestation as you draw it.

Write your intention
Make a list of words that form your intention.

_____

_____

_____

Distillation (optional)
Rewrite your words with clear intentions into a short, concise sentence.

_____

_____

_____

With thought and accuracy, think of how each word
will manifest itself as you follow these next steps.
This is action with intention. Take it slow.

1. Cross out all of the vowels in your words/sentence. Write what is left
here, making sure to keep them in their order.

_____   _____

_____   _____

_____   _____

2. Cross out any repeated letters; keep the first of each letter but remove
any duplicates.

_____   _____

_____   _____

_____   _____

3. Convert the letters to numbers then cross out any repeated numbers.
Once you assign a number to each letter, keep the first presentation of
the number and remove the duplicates. It is very important to do this
in order.

1	2	3	4	5	6	7	8	9
A	B	C	D	E	F	G	H	I
J	K	L	M	N	O	P	Q	R
S	T	U	V	W	X	Y	Z	

_____

Map It

Draw a large dot in the center of the first number to mark the beginning of your intent, then draw a line through every number's center point in the chart below in the order they appear in your number.

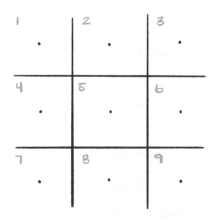

Done! Now Practice

Hone the shape into what suits you best, just make sure to do the points in order and speak your manifestation as you draw it.

Write your intention
Make a list of words that form your intention.

_____

_____

_____

Distillation (optional)
Rewrite your words with clear intentions into a short, concise sentence.

_____

_____

_____

With thought and accuracy, think of how each word
will manifest itself as you follow these next steps.
This is action with intention. Take it slow.

1. Cross out all of the vowels in your words/sentence. Write what is left here, making sure to keep them in their order.

_____   _____

_____   _____

_____   _____

2. Cross out any repeated letters; keep the first of each letter but remove any duplicates.

_____   _____

_____   _____

_____   _____

3. Convert the letters to numbers then cross out any repeated numbers. Once you assign a number to each letter, keep the first presentation of the number and remove the duplicates. It is very important to do this in order.

1	2	3	4	5	6	7	8	9
A	B	C	D	E	F	G	H	I
J	K	L	M	N	O	P	Q	R
S	T	U	V	W	X	Y	Z	

_____

Map It

Draw a large dot in the center of the first number to mark the beginning of your intent, then draw a line through every number's center point in the chart below in the order they appear in your number.

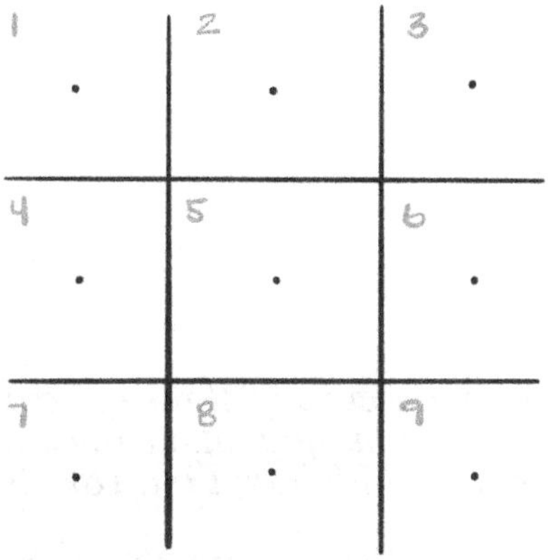

Done! Now Practice

Hone the shape into what suits you best, just make sure to do the points in order and speak your manifestation as you draw it.

Write your intention
Make a list of words that form your intention.

_____

_____

_____

Distillation (optional)
Rewrite your words with clear intentions into a short, concise sentence.

_____

_____

_____

With thought and accuracy, think of how each word
will manifest itself as you follow these next steps.
This is action with intention. Take it slow.

1. Cross out all of the vowels in your words/sentence. Write what is left here, making sure to keep them in their order.

_____   _____

_____   _____

_____   _____

2. Cross out any repeated letters; keep the first of each letter but remove any duplicates.

_____   _____

_____   _____

_____   _____

3. Convert the letters to numbers then cross out any repeated numbers. Once you assign a number to each letter, keep the first presentation of the number and remove the duplicates. It is very important to do this in order.

1	2	3	4	5	6	7	8	9
A	B	C	D	E	F	G	H	I
J	K	L	M	N	O	P	Q	R
S	T	U	V	W	X	Y	Z	

_____

Map It

Draw a large dot in the center of the first number to mark the beginning of your intent, then draw a line through every number's center point in the chart below in the order they appear in your number.

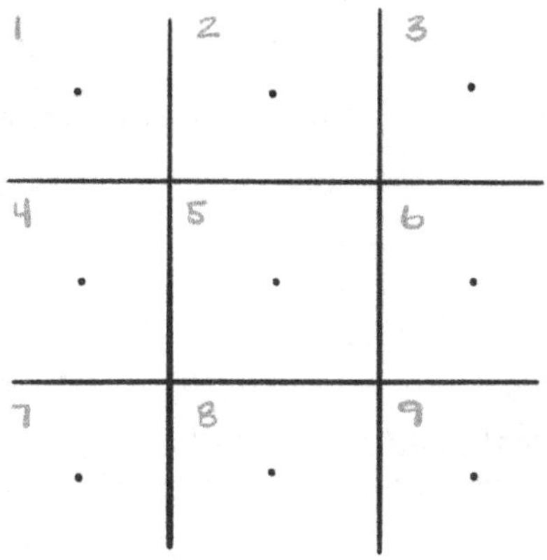

Done! Now Practice

Hone the shape into what suits you best, just make sure to do the points in order and speak your manifestation as you draw it.

Write your intention
Make a list of words that form your intention.

_____

_____

_____

Distillation (optional)
Rewrite your words with clear intentions into a short, concise sentence.

_____

_____

_____

With thought and accuracy, think of how each word
will manifest itself as you follow these next steps.
This is action with intention. Take it slow.

1. Cross out all of the vowels in your words/sentence. Write what is left here, making sure to keep them in their order.

_____   _____

_____   _____

_____   _____

2. Cross out any repeated letters; keep the first of each letter but remove any duplicates.

_____   _____

_____   _____

_____   _____

3. Convert the letters to numbers then cross out any repeated numbers. Once you assign a number to each letter, keep the first presentation of the number and remove the duplicates. It is very important to do this in order.

1	2	3	4	5	6	7	8	9
A	B	C	D	E	F	G	H	I
J	K	L	M	N	O	P	Q	R
S	T	U	V	W	X	Y	Z	

_____

Map It

Draw a large dot in the center of the first number to mark the beginning of your intent, then draw a line through every number's center point in the chart below in the order they appear in your number.

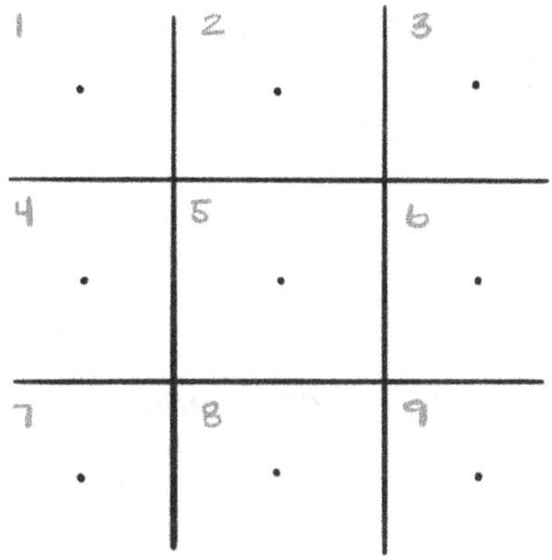

```
  1  |  2  |  3
   •  |   • |  •
_____|_____|_____
  4  |  5  |  6
   •  |   • |  •
_____|_____|_____
  7  |  8  |  9
   •  |   • |  •
```

Done! Now Practice

Hone the shape into what suits you best, just make sure to do the points in order and speak your manifestation as you draw it.

Write your intention
Make a list of words that form your intention.

_____

_____

_____

Distillation (optional)
Rewrite your words with clear intentions into a short, concise sentence.

_____

_____

_____

With thought and accuracy, think of how each word
will manifest itself as you follow these next steps.
This is action with intention. Take it slow.

1. Cross out all of the vowels in your words/sentence. Write what is left
here, making sure to keep them in their order.

_____   _____

_____   _____

_____   _____

2. Cross out any repeated letters; keep the first of each letter but remove
any duplicates.

_____   _____

_____   _____

_____   _____

3. Convert the letters to numbers then cross out any repeated numbers.
Once you assign a number to each letter, keep the first presentation of
the number and remove the duplicates. It is very important to do this
in order.

1	2	3	4	5	6	7	8	9
A	B	C	D	E	F	G	H	I
J	K	L	M	N	O	P	Q	R
S	T	U	V	W	X	Y	Z	

_____

Map It

Draw a large dot in the center of the first number to mark the beginning of your intent, then draw a line through every number's center point in the chart below in the order they appear in your number.

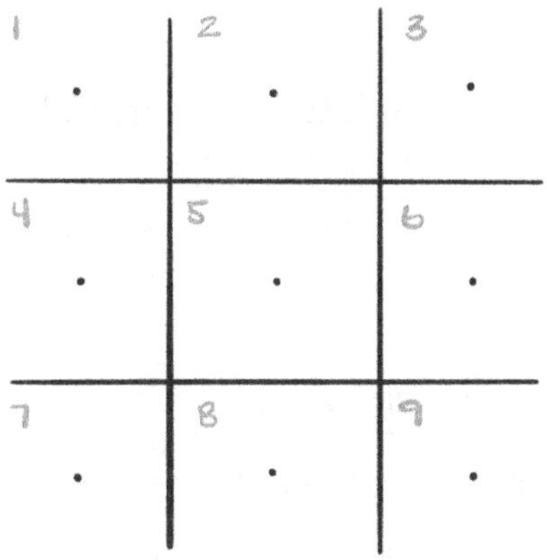

Done! Now Practice

Hone the shape into what suits you best, just make sure to do the points in order and speak your manifestation as you draw it.

Write your intention
Make a list of words that form your intention.

_____

_____

_____

Distillation (optional)
Rewrite your words with clear intentions into a short, concise sentence.

_____

_____

_____

With thought and accuracy, think of how each word
will manifest itself as you follow these next steps.
This is action with intention. Take it slow.

1. Cross out all of the vowels in your words/sentence. Write what is left here, making sure to keep them in their order.

_____   _____

_____   _____

_____   _____

2. Cross out any repeated letters; keep the first of each letter but remove any duplicates.

_____   _____

_____   _____

_____   _____

3. Convert the letters to numbers then cross out any repeated numbers. Once you assign a number to each letter, keep the first presentation of the number and remove the duplicates. It is very important to do this in order.

1	2	3	4	5	6	7	8	9
A	B	C	D	E	F	G	H	I
J	K	L	M	N	O	P	Q	R
S	T	U	V	W	X	Y	Z	

_____

Map It

Draw a large dot in the center of the first number to mark the beginning of your intent, then draw a line through every number's center point in the chart below in the order they appear in your number.

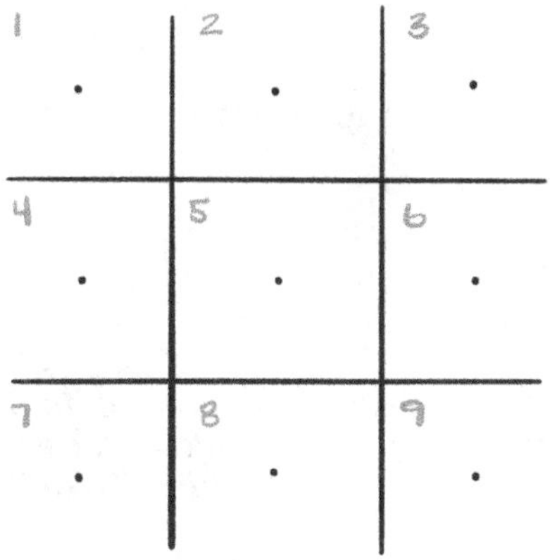

Done! Now Practice

Hone the shape into what suits you best, just make sure to do the points in order and speak your manifestation as you draw it.

Write your intention
Make a list of words that form your intention.

_____

_____

_____

Distillation (optional)
Rewrite your words with clear intentions into a short, concise sentence.

_____

_____

_____

With thought and accuracy, think of how each word
will manifest itself as you follow these next steps.
This is action with intention. Take it slow.

1. Cross out all of the vowels in your words/sentence. Write what is left here, making sure to keep them in their order.

_____   _____

_____   _____

_____   _____

2. Cross out any repeated letters; keep the first of each letter but remove any duplicates.

_____   _____

_____   _____

_____   _____

3. Convert the letters to numbers then cross out any repeated numbers. Once you assign a number to each letter, keep the first presentation of the number and remove the duplicates. It is very important to do this in order.

1	2	3	4	5	6	7	8	9
A	B	C	D	E	F	G	H	I
J	K	L	M	N	O	P	Q	R
S	T	U	V	W	X	Y	Z	

_____

Map It
Draw a large dot in the center of the first number to mark the beginning of your intent, then draw a line through every number's center point in the chart below in the order they appear in your number.

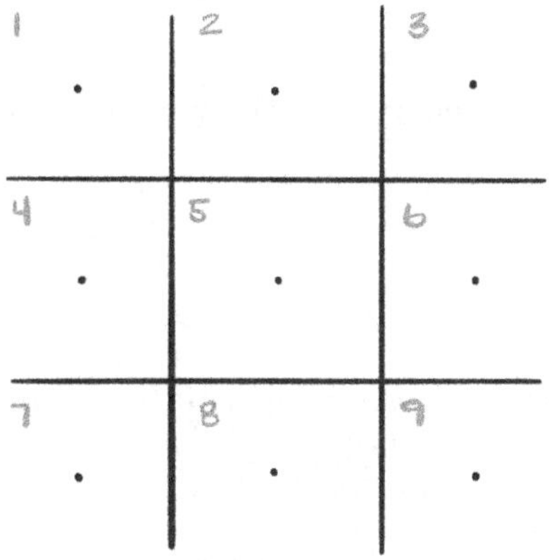

1	2	3
.	.	.
4	5	6
.	.	.
7	8	9
.	.	.

Done! Now Practice
Hone the shape into what suits you best, just make sure to do the points in order and speak your manifestation as you draw it.

Write your intention
Make a list of words that form your intention.

_____

_____

_____

Distillation (optional)
Rewrite your words with clear intentions into a short, concise sentence.

_____

_____

_____

With thought and accuracy, think of how each word
will manifest itself as you follow these next steps.
This is action with intention. Take it slow.

1. Cross out all of the vowels in your words/sentence. Write what is left here, making sure to keep them in their order.

_____   _____

_____   _____

_____   _____

2. Cross out any repeated letters; keep the first of each letter but remove any duplicates.

_____   _____

_____   _____

_____   _____

3. Convert the letters to numbers then cross out any repeated numbers. Once you assign a number to each letter, keep the first presentation of the number and remove the duplicates. It is very important to do this in order.

1	2	3	4	5	6	7	8	9
A	B	C	D	E	F	G	H	I
J	K	L	M	N	O	P	Q	R
S	T	U	V	W	X	Y	Z	

_____

Map It
Draw a large dot in the center of the first number to mark the beginning of your intent, then draw a line through every number's center point in the chart below in the order they appear in your number.

1	2	3
•	•	•
4	5	6
•	•	•
7	8	9
•	•	•

Done! Now Practice
Hone the shape into what suits you best, just make sure to do the points in order and speak your manifestation as you draw it.

Write your intention
Make a list of words that form your intention.

_____

_____

_____

Distillation (optional)
Rewrite your words with clear intentions into a short, concise sentence.

_____

_____

_____

With thought and accuracy, think of how each word
will manifest itself as you follow these next steps.
This is action with intention. Take it slow.

1. Cross out all of the vowels in your words/sentence. Write what is left here, making sure to keep them in their order.

_____   _____

_____   _____

_____   _____

2. Cross out any repeated letters; keep the first of each letter but remove any duplicates.

_____   _____

_____   _____

_____   _____

3. Convert the letters to numbers then cross out any repeated numbers. Once you assign a number to each letter, keep the first presentation of the number and remove the duplicates. It is very important to do this in order.

1	2	3	4	5	6	7	8	9
A	B	C	D	E	F	G	H	I
J	K	L	M	N	O	P	Q	R
S	T	U	V	W	X	Y	Z	

_____

Map It
Draw a large dot in the center of the first number to mark the beginning of your intent, then draw a line through every number's center point in the chart below in the order they appear in your number.

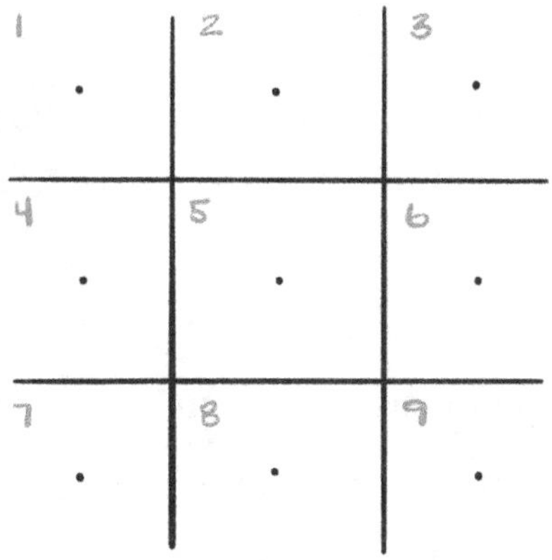

Done! Now Practice
Hone the shape into what suits you best, just make sure to do the points in order and speak your manifestation as you draw it.

Write your intention
Make a list of words that form your intention.

_____

_____

_____

Distillation (optional)
Rewrite your words with clear intentions into a short, concise sentence.

_____

_____

_____

*With thought and accuracy, think of how each word
will manifest itself as you follow these next steps.
This is action with intention. Take it slow.*

1. Cross out all of the vowels in your words/sentence. Write what is left here, making sure to keep them in their order.

_____   _____

_____   _____

_____   _____

2. Cross out any repeated letters; keep the first of each letter but remove any duplicates.

_____   _____

_____   _____

_____   _____

3. Convert the letters to numbers then cross out any repeated numbers. Once you assign a number to each letter, keep the first presentation of the number and remove the duplicates. It is very important to do this in order.

1	2	3	4	5	6	7	8	9
A	B	C	D	E	F	G	H	I
J	K	L	M	N	O	P	Q	R
S	T	U	V	W	X	Y	Z	

Map It
Draw a large dot in the center of the first number to mark the beginning of your intent, then draw a line through every number's center point in the chart below in the order they appear in your number.

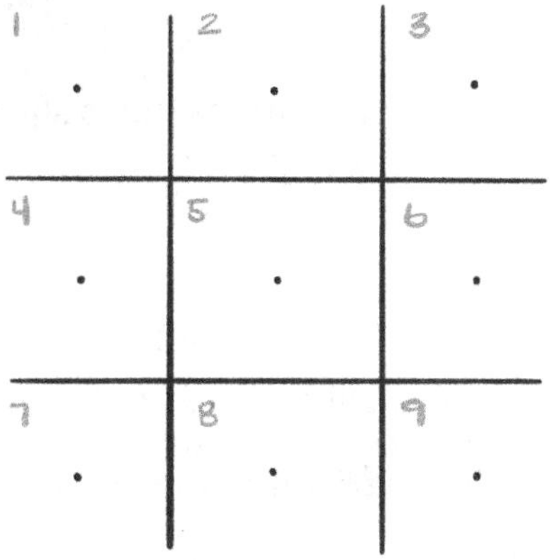

Done! Now Practice
Hone the shape into what suits you best, just make sure to do the points in order and speak your manifestation as you draw it.

Write your intention
Make a list of words that form your intention.

_____

_____

_____

Distillation (optional)
Rewrite your words with clear intentions into a short, concise sentence.

_____

_____

_____

*With thought and accuracy, think of how each word
will manifest itself as you follow these next steps.
This is action with intention. Take it slow.*

1. Cross out all of the vowels in your words/sentence. Write what is left here, making sure to keep them in their order.

_____   _____

_____   _____

_____   _____

2. Cross out any repeated letters; keep the first of each letter but remove any duplicates.

_____   _____

_____   _____

_____   _____

3. Convert the letters to numbers then cross out any repeated numbers. Once you assign a number to each letter, keep the first presentation of the number and remove the duplicates. It is very important to do this in order.

1	2	3	4	5	6	7	8	9
A	B	C	D	E	F	G	H	I
J	K	L	M	N	O	P	Q	R
S	T	U	V	W	X	Y	Z	

_____

Map It

Draw a large dot in the center of the first number to mark the beginning of your intent, then draw a line through every number's center point in the chart below in the order they appear in your number.

1	2	3
·	·	·
4	5	6
·	·	·
7	8	9
·	·	·

Done! Now Practice

Hone the shape into what suits you best, just make sure to do the points in order and speak your manifestation as you draw it.

Write your intention
Make a list of words that form your intention.

_____

_____

_____

Distillation (optional)
Rewrite your words with clear intentions into a short, concise sentence.

_____

_____

_____

*With thought and accuracy, think of how each word
will manifest itself as you follow these next steps.
This is action with intention. Take it slow.*

1. Cross out all of the vowels in your words/sentence. Write what is left here, making sure to keep them in their order.

_____   _____

_____   _____

_____   _____

2. Cross out any repeated letters; keep the first of each letter but remove any duplicates.

_____   _____

_____   _____

_____   _____

3. Convert the letters to numbers then cross out any repeated numbers. Once you assign a number to each letter, keep the first presentation of the number and remove the duplicates. It is very important to do this in order.

1	2	3	4	5	6	7	8	9
A	B	C	D	E	F	G	H	I
J	K	L	M	N	O	P	Q	R
S	T	U	V	W	X	Y	Z	

_____

Map It
Draw a large dot in the center of the first number to mark the beginning of your intent, then draw a line through every number's center point in the chart below in the order they appear in your number.

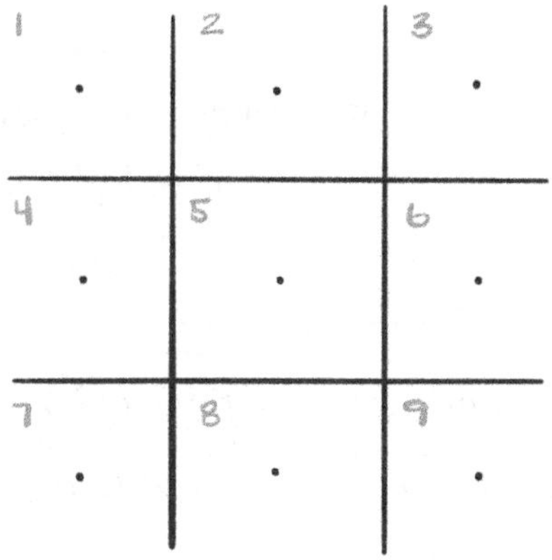

Done! Now Practice
Hone the shape into what suits you best, just make sure to do the points in order and speak your manifestation as you draw it.

Write your intention
Make a list of words that form your intention.

_____

_____

_____

Distillation (optional)
Rewrite your words with clear intentions into a short, concise sentence.

_____

_____

_____

*With thought and accuracy, think of how each word
will manifest itself as you follow these next steps.
This is action with intention. Take it slow.*

1. Cross out all of the vowels in your words/sentence. Write what is left here, making sure to keep them in their order.

_____   _____

_____   _____

_____   _____

2. Cross out any repeated letters; keep the first of each letter but remove any duplicates.

_____   _____

_____   _____

_____   _____

3. Convert the letters to numbers then cross out any repeated numbers. Once you assign a number to each letter, keep the first presentation of the number and remove the duplicates. It is very important to do this in order.

1	2	3	4	5	6	7	8	9
A	B	C	D	E	F	G	H	I
J	K	L	M	N	O	P	Q	R
S	T	U	V	W	X	Y	Z	

_____

Map It

Draw a large dot in the center of the first number to mark the beginning of your intent, then draw a line through every number's center point in the chart below in the order they appear in your number.

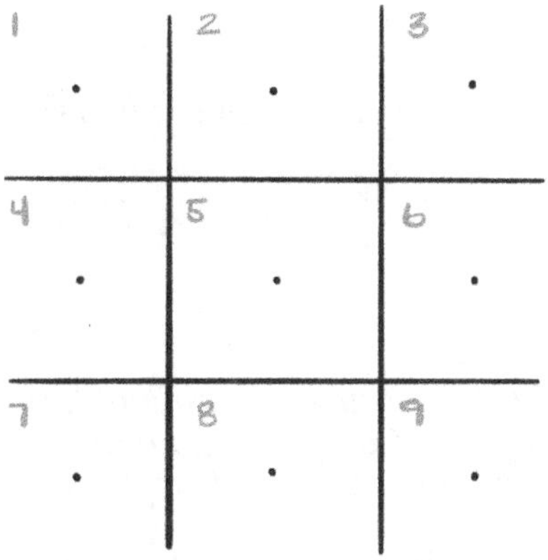

Done! Now Practice

Hone the shape into what suits you best, just make sure to do the points in order and speak your manifestation as you draw it.

Write your intention
Make a list of words that form your intention.

_____

_____

_____

Distillation (optional)
Rewrite your words with clear intentions into a short, concise sentence.

_____

_____

_____

*With thought and accuracy, think of how each word
will manifest itself as you follow these next steps.
This is action with intention. Take it slow.*

1. Cross out all of the vowels in your words/sentence. Write what is left here, making sure to keep them in their order.

_____   _____

_____   _____

_____   _____

2. Cross out any repeated letters; keep the first of each letter but remove any duplicates.

_____   _____

_____   _____

_____   _____

3. Convert the letters to numbers then cross out any repeated numbers. Once you assign a number to each letter, keep the first presentation of the number and remove the duplicates. It is very important to do this in order.

1	2	3	4	5	6	7	8	9
A	B	C	D	E	F	G	H	I
J	K	L	M	N	O	P	Q	R
S	T	U	V	W	X	Y	Z	

_____

170

Map It

Draw a large dot in the center of the first number to mark the beginning of your intent, then draw a line through every number's center point in the chart below in the order they appear in your number.

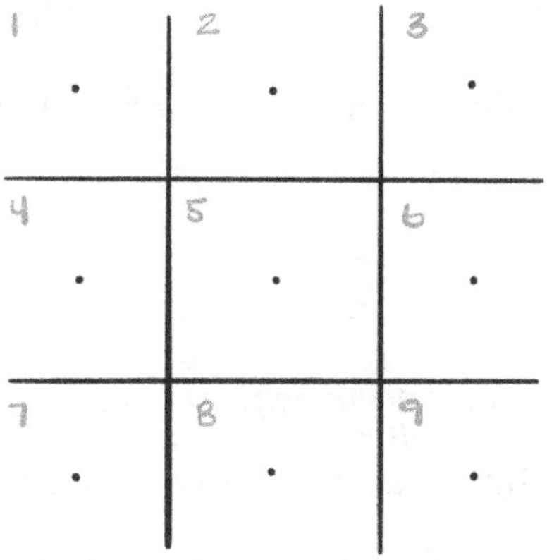

Done! Now Practice

Hone the shape into what suits you best, just make sure to do the points in order and speak your manifestation as you draw it.

Write your intention
Make a list of words that form your intention.

_____

_____

_____

Distillation (optional)
Rewrite your words with clear intentions into a short, concise sentence.

_____

_____

_____

With thought and accuracy, think of how each word
will manifest itself as you follow these next steps.
This is action with intention. Take it slow.

1. Cross out all of the vowels in your words/sentence. Write what is left here, making sure to keep them in their order.

_____   _____

_____   _____

_____   _____

2. Cross out any repeated letters; keep the first of each letter but remove any duplicates.

_____   _____

_____   _____

_____   _____

3. Convert the letters to numbers then cross out any repeated numbers. Once you assign a number to each letter, keep the first presentation of the number and remove the duplicates. It is very important to do this in order.

1	2	3	4	5	6	7	8	9
A	B	C	D	E	F	G	H	I
J	K	L	M	N	O	P	Q	R
S	T	U	V	W	X	Y	Z	

_____

172

Map It

Draw a large dot in the center of the first number to mark the beginning of your intent, then draw a line through every number's center point in the chart below in the order they appear in your number.

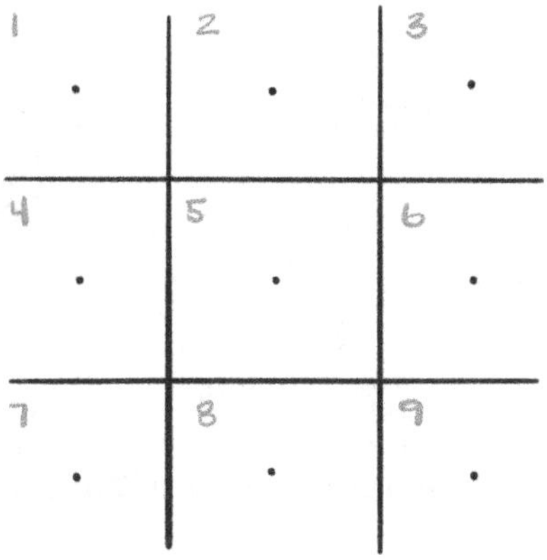

Done! Now Practice

Hone the shape into what suits you best, just make sure to do the points in order and speak your manifestation as you draw it.

Write your intention
Make a list of words that form your intention.

_____

_____

_____

Distillation (optional)
Rewrite your words with clear intentions into a short, concise sentence.

_____

_____

_____

*With thought and accuracy, think of how each word
will manifest itself as you follow these next steps.
This is action with intention. Take it slow.*

1. Cross out all of the vowels in your words/sentence. Write what is left
here, making sure to keep them in their order.

_____   _____

_____   _____

_____   _____

2. Cross out any repeated letters; keep the first of each letter but remove
any duplicates.

_____   _____

_____   _____

_____   _____

3. Convert the letters to numbers then cross out any repeated numbers.
Once you assign a number to each letter, keep the first presentation of
the number and remove the duplicates. It is very important to do this
in order.

1	2	3	4	5	6	7	8	9
A	B	C	D	E	F	G	H	I
J	K	L	M	N	O	P	Q	R
S	T	U	V	W	X	Y	Z	

_____

Map It
Draw a large dot in the center of the first number to mark the beginning of your intent, then draw a line through every number's center point in the chart below in the order they appear in your number.

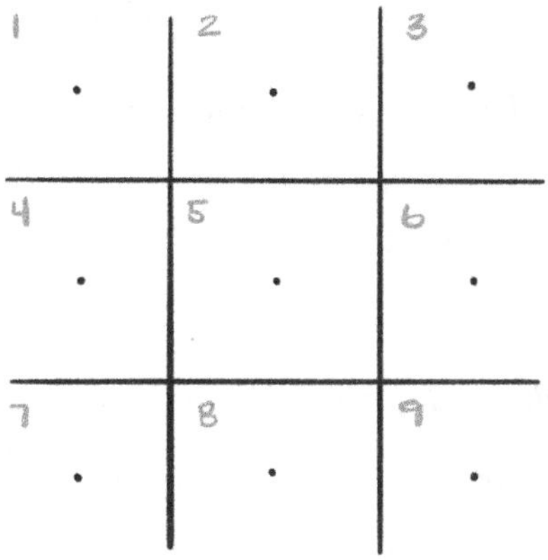

Done! Now Practice
Hone the shape into what suits you best, just make sure to do the points in order and speak your manifestation as you draw it.

Write your intention
Make a list of words that form your intention.

_____

_____

_____

Distillation (optional)
Rewrite your words with clear intentions into a short, concise sentence.

_____

_____

_____

With thought and accuracy, think of how each word
will manifest itself as you follow these next steps.
This is action with intention. Take it slow.

1. Cross out all of the vowels in your words/sentence. Write what is left here, making sure to keep them in their order.

_____   _____

_____   _____

_____   _____

2. Cross out any repeated letters; keep the first of each letter but remove any duplicates.

_____   _____

_____   _____

_____   _____

3. Convert the letters to numbers then cross out any repeated numbers. Once you assign a number to each letter, keep the first presentation of the number and remove the duplicates. It is very important to do this in order.

1	2	3	4	5	6	7	8	9
A	B	C	D	E	F	G	H	I
J	K	L	M	N	O	P	Q	R
S	T	U	V	W	X	Y	Z	

_____

Map It

Draw a large dot in the center of the first number to mark the beginning of your intent, then draw a line through every number's center point in the chart below in the order they appear in your number.

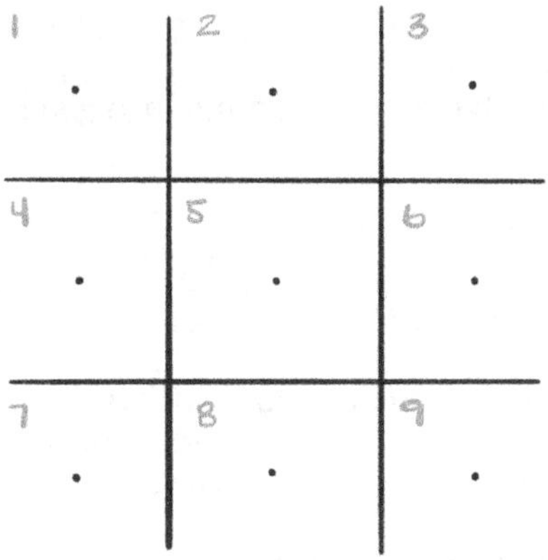

Done! Now Practice

Hone the shape into what suits you best, just make sure to do the points in order and speak your manifestation as you draw it.

Write your intention
Make a list of words that form your intention.

_____

_____

_____

Distillation (optional)
Rewrite your words with clear intentions into a short, concise sentence.

_____

_____

_____

With thought and accuracy, think of how each word
will manifest itself as you follow these next steps.
This is action with intention. Take it slow.

1. Cross out all of the vowels in your words/sentence. Write what is left here, making sure to keep them in their order.

_____   _____

_____   _____

_____   _____

2. Cross out any repeated letters; keep the first of each letter but remove any duplicates.

_____   _____

_____   _____

_____   _____

3. Convert the letters to numbers then cross out any repeated numbers. Once you assign a number to each letter, keep the first presentation of the number and remove the duplicates. It is very important to do this in order.

1	2	3	4	5	6	7	8	9
A	B	C	D	E	F	G	H	I
J	K	L	M	N	O	P	Q	R
S	T	U	V	W	X	Y	Z	

_____

Map It
Draw a large dot in the center of the first number to mark the beginning of your intent, then draw a line through every number's center point in the chart below in the order they appear in your number.

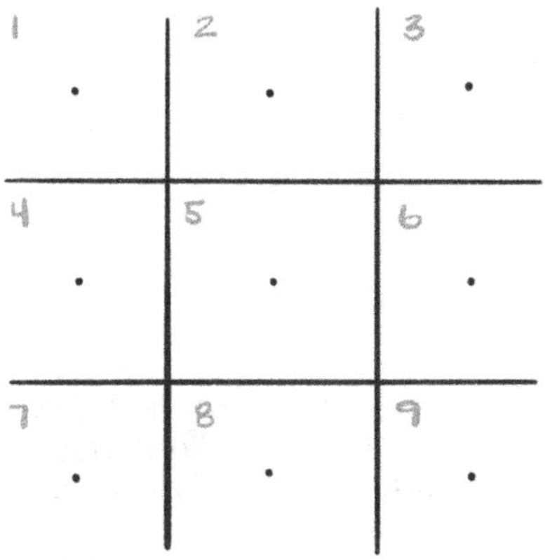

Done! Now Practice
Hone the shape into what suits you best, just make sure to do the points in order and speak your manifestation as you draw it.

Write your intention
Make a list of words that form your intention.

_____

_____

_____

Distillation (optional)
Rewrite your words with clear intentions into a short, concise sentence.

_____

_____

_____

*With thought and accuracy, think of how each word
will manifest itself as you follow these next steps.
This is action with intention. Take it slow.*

1. Cross out all of the vowels in your words/sentence. Write what is left
here, making sure to keep them in their order.

_____   _____

_____   _____

_____   _____

2. Cross out any repeated letters; keep the first of each letter but remove
any duplicates.

_____   _____

_____   _____

_____   _____

3. Convert the letters to numbers then cross out any repeated numbers.
Once you assign a number to each letter, keep the first presentation of
the number and remove the duplicates. It is very important to do this
in order.

1	2	3	4	5	6	7	8	9
A	B	C	D	E	F	G	H	I
J	K	L	M	N	O	P	Q	R
S	T	U	V	W	X	Y	Z	

_____

Map It
Draw a large dot in the center of the first number to mark the beginning of your intent, then draw a line through every number's center point in the chart below in the order they appear in your number.

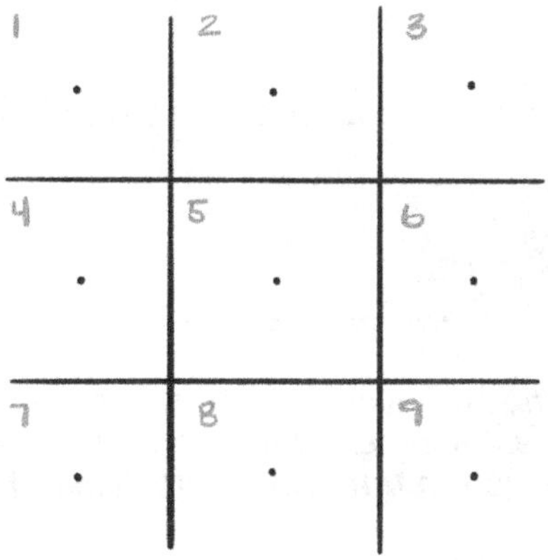

Done! Now Practice
Hone the shape into what suits you best, just make sure to do the points in order and speak your manifestation as you draw it.

Write your intention
Make a list of words that form your intention.

_____

_____

_____

Distillation (optional)
Rewrite your words with clear intentions into a short, concise sentence.

_____

_____

_____

With thought and accuracy, think of how each word
will manifest itself as you follow these next steps.
This is action with intention. Take it slow.

1. Cross out all of the vowels in your words/sentence. Write what is left here, making sure to keep them in their order.

_____   _____

_____   _____

_____   _____

2. Cross out any repeated letters; keep the first of each letter but remove any duplicates.

_____   _____

_____   _____

_____   _____

3. Convert the letters to numbers then cross out any repeated numbers. Once you assign a number to each letter, keep the first presentation of the number and remove the duplicates. It is very important to do this in order.

1	2	3	4	5	6	7	8	9
A	B	C	D	E	F	G	H	I
J	K	L	M	N	O	P	Q	R
S	T	U	V	W	X	Y	Z	

_____

Map It
Draw a large dot in the center of the first number to mark the beginning of your intent, then draw a line through every number's center point in the chart below in the order they appear in your number.

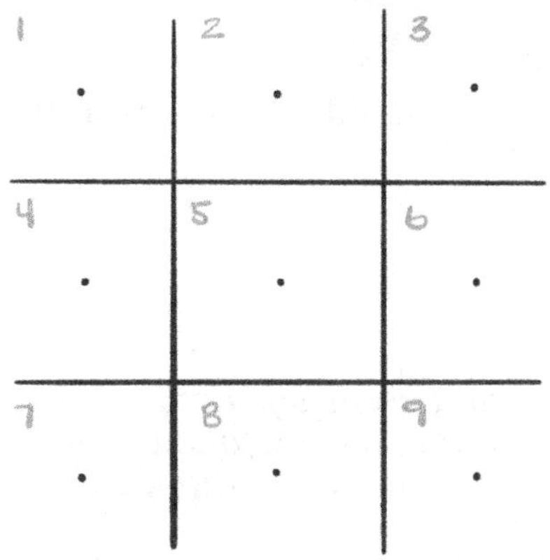

Done! Now Practice
Hone the shape into what suits you best, just make sure to do the points in order and speak your manifestation as you draw it.

Write your intention
Make a list of words that form your intention.

_____

_____

_____

Distillation (optional)
Rewrite your words with clear intentions into a short, concise sentence.

_____

_____

_____

With thought and accuracy, think of how each word
will manifest itself as you follow these next steps.
This is action with intention. Take it slow.

1. Cross out all of the vowels in your words/sentence. Write what is left here, making sure to keep them in their order.

_____   _____

_____   _____

_____   _____

2. Cross out any repeated letters; keep the first of each letter but remove any duplicates.

_____   _____

_____   _____

_____   _____

3. Convert the letters to numbers then cross out any repeated numbers. Once you assign a number to each letter, keep the first presentation of the number and remove the duplicates. It is very important to do this in order.

1	2	3	4	5	6	7	8	9
A	B	C	D	E	F	G	H	I
J	K	L	M	N	O	P	Q	R
S	T	U	V	W	X	Y	Z	

_____

Map It
Draw a large dot in the center of the first number to mark the beginning of your intent, then draw a line through every number's center point in the chart below in the order they appear in your number.

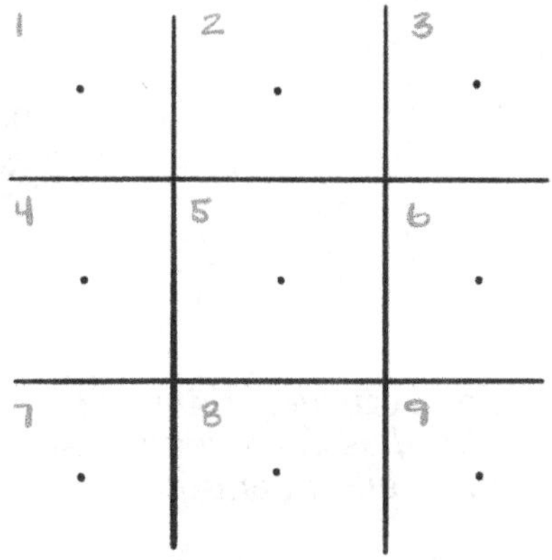

Done! Now Practice
Hone the shape into what suits you best, just make sure to do the points in order and speak your manifestation as you draw it.

Write your intention
Make a list of words that form your intention.

_____

_____

_____

Distillation (optional)
Rewrite your words with clear intentions into a short, concise sentence.

_____

_____

_____

With thought and accuracy, think of how each word
will manifest itself as you follow these next steps.
This is action with intention. Take it slow.

1. Cross out all of the vowels in your words/sentence. Write what is left here, making sure to keep them in their order.

_____   _____

_____   _____

_____   _____

2. Cross out any repeated letters; keep the first of each letter but remove any duplicates.

_____   _____

_____   _____

_____   _____

3. Convert the letters to numbers then cross out any repeated numbers. Once you assign a number to each letter, keep the first presentation of the number and remove the duplicates. It is very important to do this in order.

1	2	3	4	5	6	7	8	9
A	B	C	D	E	F	G	H	I
J	K	L	M	N	O	P	Q	R
S	T	U	V	W	X	Y	Z	

_____

Map It
Draw a large dot in the center of the first number to mark the beginning of your intent, then draw a line through every number's center point in the chart below in the order they appear in your number.

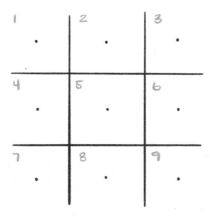

Done! Now Practice
Hone the shape into what suits you best, just make sure to do the points in order and speak your manifestation as you draw it.

Write your intention
Make a list of words that form your intention.

_____

_____

_____

Distillation (optional)
Rewrite your words with clear intentions into a short, concise sentence.

_____

_____

_____

With thought and accuracy, think of how each word
will manifest itself as you follow these next steps.
This is action with intention. Take it slow.

1. Cross out all of the vowels in your words/sentence. Write what is left here, making sure to keep them in their order.

_____   _____

_____   _____

_____   _____

2. Cross out any repeated letters; keep the first of each letter but remove any duplicates.

_____   _____

_____   _____

_____   _____

3. Convert the letters to numbers then cross out any repeated numbers. Once you assign a number to each letter, keep the first presentation of the number and remove the duplicates. It is very important to do this in order.

1	2	3	4	5	6	7	8	9
A	B	C	D	E	F	G	H	I
J	K	L	M	N	O	P	Q	R
S	T	U	V	W	X	Y	Z	

_____

Map It
Draw a large dot in the center of the first number to mark the beginning of your intent, then draw a line through every number's center point in the chart below in the order they appear in your number.

```
  1     |   2     |   3
        |         |
    •   |     •   |     •
  _____|_____|_____
  4     |   5     |   6
        |         |
    •   |     •   |     •
  _____|_____|_____
  7     |   8     |   9
        |         |
    •   |     •   |     •
        |         |
```

Done! Now Practice
Hone the shape into what suits you best, just make sure to do the points in order and speak your manifestation as you draw it.

Write your intention
Make a list of words that form your intention.

_____

_____

_____

Distillation (optional)
Rewrite your words with clear intentions into a short, concise sentence.

_____

_____

_____

*With thought and accuracy, think of how each word
will manifest itself as you follow these next steps.
This is action with intention. Take it slow.*

1. Cross out all of the vowels in your words/sentence. Write what is left here, making sure to keep them in their order.

_____   _____

_____   _____

_____   _____

2. Cross out any repeated letters; keep the first of each letter but remove any duplicates.

_____   _____

_____   _____

_____   _____

3. Convert the letters to numbers then cross out any repeated numbers. Once you assign a number to each letter, keep the first presentation of the number and remove the duplicates. It is very important to do this in order.

1	2	3	4	5	6	7	8	9
A	B	C	D	E	F	G	H	I
J	K	L	M	N	O	P	Q	R
S	T	U	V	W	X	Y	Z	

_____

Map It

Draw a large dot in the center of the first number to mark the beginning of your intent, then draw a line through every number's center point in the chart below in the order they appear in your number.

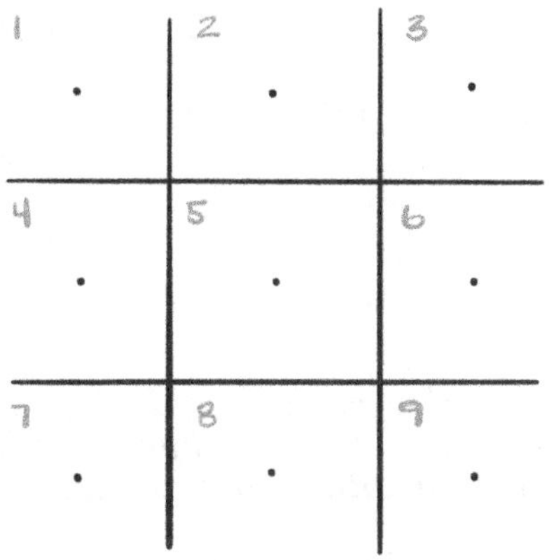

Done! Now Practice

Hone the shape into what suits you best, just make sure to do the points in order and speak your manifestation as you draw it.

Write your intention
Make a list of words that form your intention.

_____

_____

_____

Distillation (optional)
Rewrite your words with clear intentions into a short, concise sentence.

_____

_____

_____

With thought and accuracy, think of how each word
will manifest itself as you follow these next steps.
This is action with intention. Take it slow.

1. Cross out all of the vowels in your words/sentence. Write what is left here, making sure to keep them in their order.

_____   _____

_____   _____

_____   _____

2. Cross out any repeated letters; keep the first of each letter but remove any duplicates.

_____   _____

_____   _____

_____   _____

3. Convert the letters to numbers then cross out any repeated numbers. Once you assign a number to each letter, keep the first presentation of the number and remove the duplicates. It is very important to do this in order.

1	2	3	4	5	6	7	8	9
A	B	C	D	E	F	G	H	I
J	K	L	M	N	O	P	Q	R
S	T	U	V	W	X	Y	Z	

_____

Map It
Draw a large dot in the center of the first number to mark the beginning
of your intent, then draw a line through every number's center point in
the chart below in the order they appear in your number.

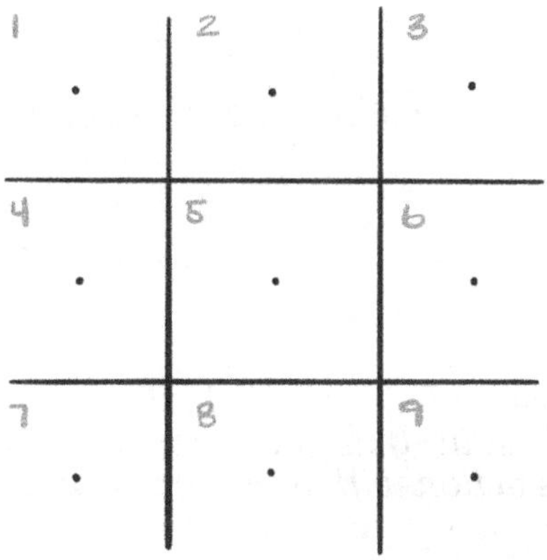

1	2	3
•	•	•
4	5	6
•	•	•
7	8	9
•	•	•

Done! Now Practice
Hone the shape into what suits you best, just make sure to do the points
in order and speak your manifestation as you draw it.

Write your intention
Make a list of words that form your intention.

_____

_____

_____

Distillation (optional)
Rewrite your words with clear intentions into a short, concise sentence.

_____

_____

_____

*With thought and accuracy, think of how each word
will manifest itself as you follow these next steps.
This is action with intention. Take it slow.*

1. Cross out all of the vowels in your words/sentence. Write what is left here, making sure to keep them in their order.

_____   _____

_____   _____

_____   _____

2. Cross out any repeated letters; keep the first of each letter but remove any duplicates.

_____   _____

_____   _____

_____   _____

3. Convert the letters to numbers then cross out any repeated numbers. Once you assign a number to each letter, keep the first presentation of the number and remove the duplicates. It is very important to do this in order.

1	2	3	4	5	6	7	8	9
A	B	C	D	E	F	G	H	I
J	K	L	M	N	O	P	Q	R
S	T	U	V	W	X	Y	Z	

_____

Map It

Draw a large dot in the center of the first number to mark the beginning of your intent, then draw a line through every number's center point in the chart below in the order they appear in your number.

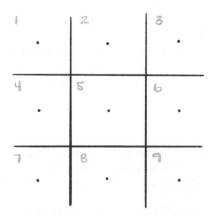

Done! Now Practice

Hone the shape into what suits you best, just make sure to do the points in order and speak your manifestation as you draw it.

Write your intention
Make a list of words that form your intention.

_____

_____

_____

Distillation (optional)
Rewrite your words with clear intentions into a short, concise sentence.

_____

_____

_____

With thought and accuracy, think of how each word
will manifest itself as you follow these next steps.
This is action with intention. Take it slow.

1. Cross out all of the vowels in your words/sentence. Write what is left here, making sure to keep them in their order.

_____   _____

_____   _____

_____   _____

2. Cross out any repeated letters; keep the first of each letter but remove any duplicates.

_____   _____

_____   _____

_____   _____

3. Convert the letters to numbers then cross out any repeated numbers. Once you assign a number to each letter, keep the first presentation of the number and remove the duplicates. It is very important to do this in order.

1	2	3	4	5	6	7	8	9
A	B	C	D	E	F	G	H	I
J	K	L	M	N	O	P	Q	R
S	T	U	V	W	X	Y	Z	

_____

Map It

Draw a large dot in the center of the first number to mark the beginning of your intent, then draw a line through every number's center point in the chart below in the order they appear in your number.

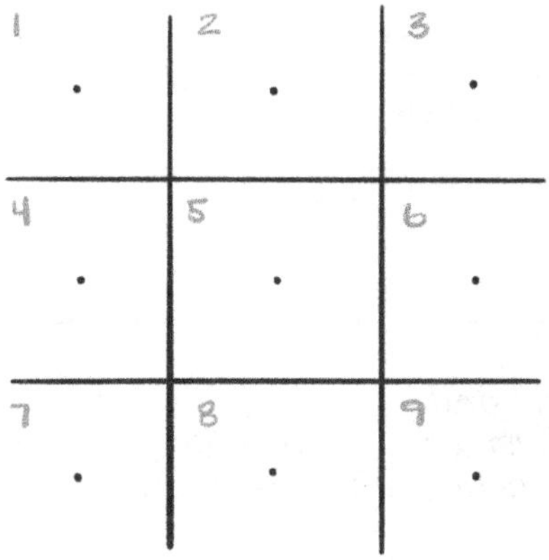

Done! Now Practice

Hone the shape into what suits you best, just make sure to do the points in order and speak your manifestation as you draw it.

Write your intention
Make a list of words that form your intention.

_____

_____

_____

Distillation (optional)
Rewrite your words with clear intentions into a short, concise sentence.

_____

_____

_____

With thought and accuracy, think of how each word
will manifest itself as you follow these next steps.
This is action with intention. Take it slow.

1. Cross out all of the vowels in your words/sentence. Write what is left here, making sure to keep them in their order.

_____   _____

_____   _____

_____

2. Cross out any repeated letters; keep the first of each letter but remove any duplicates.

_____   _____

_____   _____

_____   _____

3. Convert the letters to numbers then cross out any repeated numbers. Once you assign a number to each letter, keep the first presentation of the number and remove the duplicates. It is very important to do this in order.

1	2	3	4	5	6	7	8	9
A	B	C	D	E	F	G	H	I
J	K	L	M	N	O	P	Q	R
S	T	U	V	W	X	Y	Z	

_____

Map It
Draw a large dot in the center of the first number to mark the beginning
of your intent, then draw a line through every number's center point in
the chart below in the order they appear in your number.

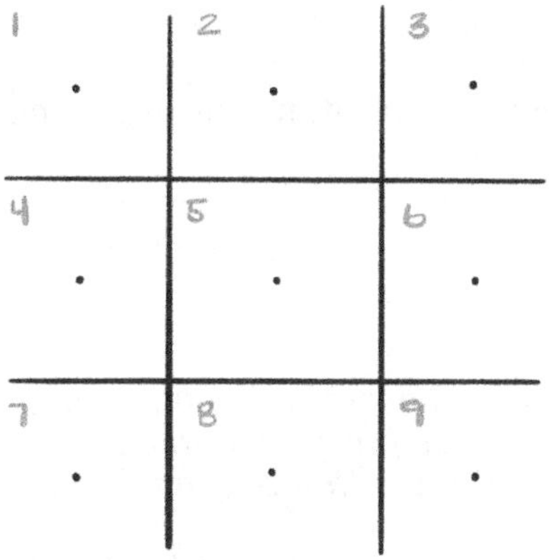

Done! Now Practice
Hone the shape into what suits you best, just make sure to do the points
in order and speak your manifestation as you draw it.

Write your intention
Make a list of words that form your intention.

_____

_____

_____

Distillation (optional)
Rewrite your words with clear intentions into a short, concise sentence.

_____

_____

_____

With thought and accuracy, think of how each word
will manifest itself as you follow these next steps.
This is action with intention. Take it slow.

1. Cross out all of the vowels in your words/sentence. Write what is left here, making sure to keep them in their order.

_____   _____

_____   _____

_____   _____

2. Cross out any repeated letters; keep the first of each letter but remove any duplicates.

_____   _____

_____   _____

_____   _____

3. Convert the letters to numbers then cross out any repeated numbers. Once you assign a number to each letter, keep the first presentation of the number and remove the duplicates. It is very important to do this in order.

1	2	3	4	5	6	7	8	9
A	B	C	D	E	F	G	H	I
J	K	L	M	N	O	P	Q	R
S	T	U	V	W	X	Y	Z	

_____

Map It
Draw a large dot in the center of the first number to mark the beginning of your intent, then draw a line through every number's center point in the chart below in the order they appear in your number.

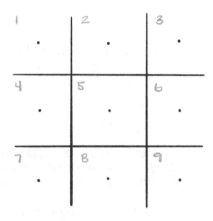

Done! Now Practice
Hone the shape into what suits you best, just make sure to do the points in order and speak your manifestation as you draw it.

Write your intention
Make a list of words that form your intention.

Distillation (optional)
Rewrite your words with clear intentions into a short, concise sentence.

With thought and accuracy, think of how each word
will manifest itself as you follow these next steps.
This is action with intention. Take it slow.

1. Cross out all of the vowels in your words/sentence. Write what is left here, making sure to keep them in their order.

_____	_____
_____	_____
_____	_____

2. Cross out any repeated letters; keep the first of each letter but remove any duplicates.

_____	_____
_____	_____
_____	_____

3. Convert the letters to numbers then cross out any repeated numbers. Once you assign a number to each letter, keep the first presentation of the number and remove the duplicates. It is very important to do this in order.

1	2	3	4	5	6	7	8	9
A	B	C	D	E	F	G	H	I
J	K	L	M	N	O	P	Q	R
S	T	U	V	W	X	Y	Z	

Map It
Draw a large dot in the center of the first number to mark the beginning of your intent, then draw a line through every number's center point in the chart below in the order they appear in your number.

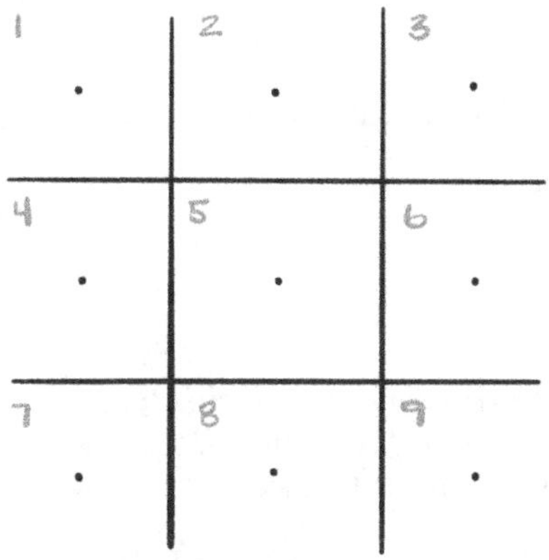

1	2	3
·	·	·
4	5	6
·	·	·
7	8	9
·	·	·

Done! Now Practice
Hone the shape into what suits you best, just make sure to do the points in order and speak your manifestation as you draw it.

Write your intention
Make a list of words that form your intention.

_____

_____

_____

Distillation (optional)
Rewrite your words with clear intentions into a short, concise sentence.

_____

_____

_____

With thought and accuracy, think of how each word
will manifest itself as you follow these next steps.
This is action with intention. Take it slow.

1. Cross out all of the vowels in your words/sentence. Write what is left here, making sure to keep them in their order.

_____   _____

_____   _____

_____   _____

2. Cross out any repeated letters; keep the first of each letter but remove any duplicates.

_____   _____

_____   _____

_____   _____

3. Convert the letters to numbers then cross out any repeated numbers. Once you assign a number to each letter, keep the first presentation of the number and remove the duplicates. It is very important to do this in order.

1	2	3	4	5	6	7	8	9
A	B	C	D	E	F	G	H	I
J	K	L	M	N	O	P	Q	R
S	T	U	V	W	X	Y	Z	

_____

Map It

Draw a large dot in the center of the first number to mark the beginning of your intent, then draw a line through every number's center point in the chart below in the order they appear in your number.

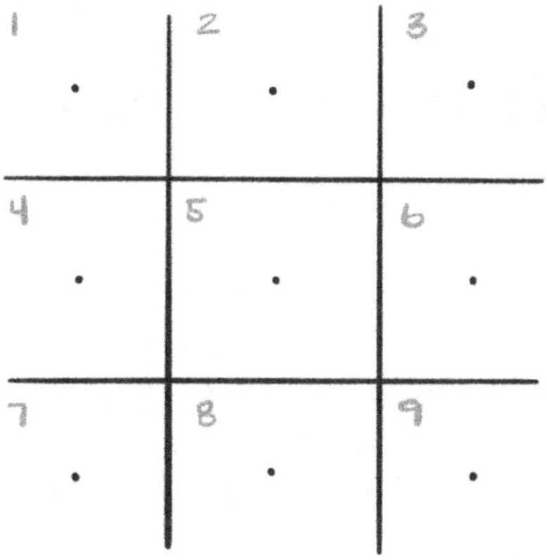

Done! Now Practice

Hone the shape into what suits you best, just make sure to do the points in order and speak your manifestation as you draw it.

Write your intention
Make a list of words that form your intention.

_____

_____

_____

Distillation (optional)
Rewrite your words with clear intentions into a short, concise sentence.

_____

_____

_____

With thought and accuracy, think of how each word
will manifest itself as you follow these next steps.
This is action with intention. Take it slow.

1. Cross out all of the vowels in your words/sentence. Write what is left here, making sure to keep them in their order.

_____   _____

_____   _____

_____   _____

2. Cross out any repeated letters; keep the first of each letter but remove any duplicates.

_____   _____

_____   _____

_____   _____

3. Convert the letters to numbers then cross out any repeated numbers. Once you assign a number to each letter, keep the first presentation of the number and remove the duplicates. It is very important to do this in order.

1	2	3	4	5	6	7	8	9
A	B	C	D	E	F	G	H	I
J	K	L	M	N	O	P	Q	R
S	T	U	V	W	X	Y	Z	

_____

Map It
Draw a large dot in the center of the first number to mark the beginning
of your intent, then draw a line through every number's center point in
the chart below in the order they appear in your number.

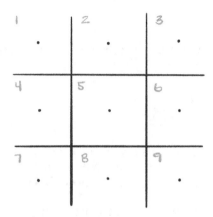

Done! Now Practice
Hone the shape into what suits you best, just make sure to do the points
in order and speak your manifestation as you draw it.

Write your intention
Make a list of words that form your intention.

_____

_____

_____

Distillation (optional)
Rewrite your words with clear intentions into a short, concise sentence.

_____

_____

_____

With thought and accuracy, think of how each word
will manifest itself as you follow these next steps.
This is action with intention. Take it slow.

1. Cross out all of the vowels in your words/sentence. Write what is left here, making sure to keep them in their order.

_____   _____

_____   _____

_____   _____

2. Cross out any repeated letters; keep the first of each letter but remove any duplicates.

_____   _____

_____   _____

_____   _____

3. Convert the letters to numbers then cross out any repeated numbers. Once you assign a number to each letter, keep the first presentation of the number and remove the duplicates. It is very important to do this in order.

1	2	3	4	5	6	7	8	9
A	B	C	D	E	F	G	H	I
J	K	L	M	N	O	P	Q	R
S	T	U	V	W	X	Y	Z	

_____

Map It

Draw a large dot in the center of the first number to mark the beginning of your intent, then draw a line through every number's center point in the chart below in the order they appear in your number.

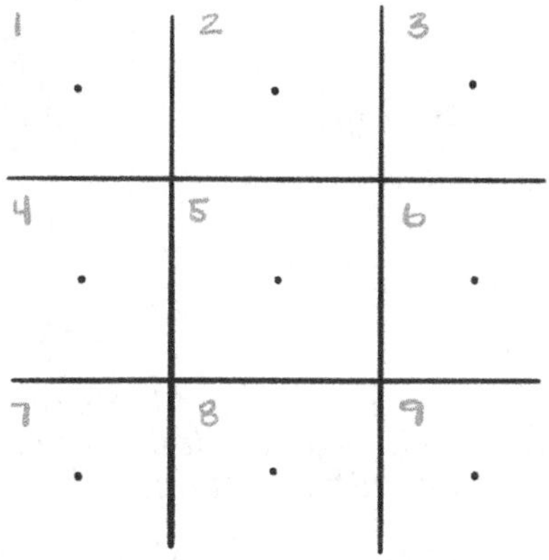

Done! Now Practice

Hone the shape into what suits you best, just make sure to do the points in order and speak your manifestation as you draw it.

Write your intention
Make a list of words that form your intention.

_____

_____

_____

Distillation (optional)
Rewrite your words with clear intentions into a short, concise sentence.

_____

_____

_____

With thought and accuracy, think of how each word
will manifest itself as you follow these next steps.
This is action with intention. Take it slow.

1. Cross out all of the vowels in your words/sentence. Write what is left here, making sure to keep them in their order.

_____   _____

_____   _____

_____   _____

2. Cross out any repeated letters; keep the first of each letter but remove any duplicates.

_____   _____

_____   _____

_____   _____

3. Convert the letters to numbers then cross out any repeated numbers. Once you assign a number to each letter, keep the first presentation of the number and remove the duplicates. It is very important to do this in order.

1	2	3	4	5	6	7	8	9
A	B	C	D	E	F	G	H	I
J	K	L	M	N	O	P	Q	R
S	T	U	V	W	X	Y	Z	

_____

Map It
Draw a large dot in the center of the first number to mark the beginning of your intent, then draw a line through every number's center point in the chart below in the order they appear in your number.

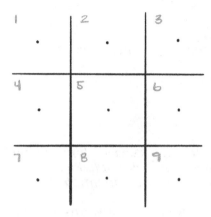

Done! Now Practice
Hone the shape into what suits you best, just make sure to do the points in order and speak your manifestation as you draw it.

Write your intention
Make a list of words that form your intention.

_____

_____

_____

Distillation (optional)
Rewrite your words with clear intentions into a short, concise sentence.

_____

_____

_____

With thought and accuracy, think of how each word
will manifest itself as you follow these next steps.
This is action with intention. Take it slow.

1. Cross out all of the vowels in your words/sentence. Write what is left here, making sure to keep them in their order.

_____   _____

_____   _____

_____   _____

2. Cross out any repeated letters; keep the first of each letter but remove any duplicates.

_____   _____

_____   _____

_____   _____

3. Convert the letters to numbers then cross out any repeated numbers. Once you assign a number to each letter, keep the first presentation of the number and remove the duplicates. It is very important to do this in order.

1	2	3	4	5	6	7	8	9
A	B	C	D	E	F	G	H	I
J	K	L	M	N	O	P	Q	R
S	T	U	V	W	X	Y	Z	

_____

Map It
Draw a large dot in the center of the first number to mark the beginning
of your intent, then draw a line through every number's center point in
the chart below in the order they appear in your number.

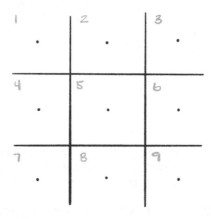

Done! Now Practice
Hone the shape into what suits you best, just make sure to do the points
in order and speak your manifestation as you draw it.

Write your intention

Make a list of words that form your intention.

_____

_____

_____

Distillation (optional)

Rewrite your words with clear intentions into a short, concise sentence.

_____

_____

_____

With thought and accuracy, think of how each word
will manifest itself as you follow these next steps.
This is action with intention. Take it slow.

1. Cross out all of the vowels in your words/sentence. Write what is left here, making sure to keep them in their order.

_____   _____

_____   _____

_____   _____

2. Cross out any repeated letters; keep the first of each letter but remove any duplicates.

_____   _____

_____   _____

_____   _____

3. Convert the letters to numbers then cross out any repeated numbers. Once you assign a number to each letter, keep the first presentation of the number and remove the duplicates. It is very important to do this in order.

1	2	3	4	5	6	7	8	9
A	B	C	D	E	F	G	H	I
J	K	L	M	N	O	P	Q	R
S	T	U	V	W	X	Y	Z	

_____

Map It

Draw a large dot in the center of the first number to mark the beginning of your intent, then draw a line through every number's center point in the chart below in the order they appear in your number.

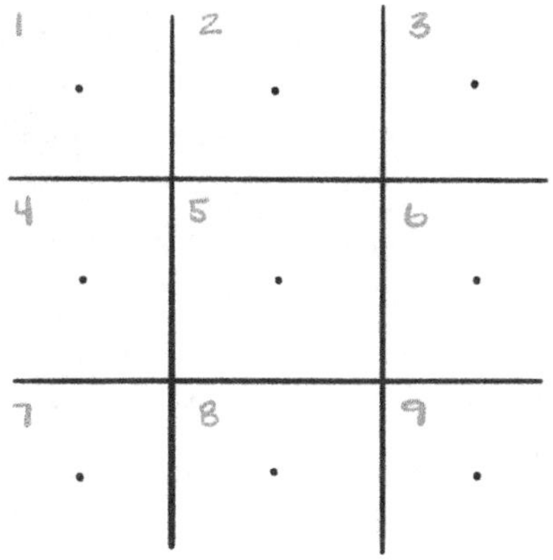

Done! Now Practice

Hone the shape into what suits you best, just make sure to do the points in order and speak your manifestation as you draw it.

INDEX

PAGE NO.   SIGIL / INTENT

_____   _____

_____   _____

_____   _____

_____   _____

_____   _____

_____   _____

_____   _____

_____   _____

_____   _____

_____   _____

_____   _____

_____   _____

_____   _____

_____   _____

_____   _____

_____   _____

_____   _____

_____   _____

_____   _____

_____   _____

_____   _____

INDEX

PAGE NO.　　SIGIL / INTENT

INDEX

PAGE NO.   SIGIL / INTENT

CPSIA information can be obtained
at www.ICGtesting.com
Printed in the USA
BVHW041037220921
617191BV00019B/1711

9 781734 510492